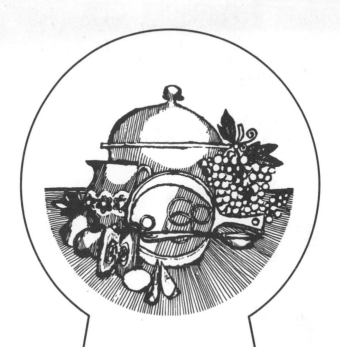

COOKING SECRETS
❧ YOUR MOTHER ❧
NEVER TOLD YOU !

TABLE OF CONTENTS

COOKING SECRETS YOUR MOTHER NEVER TOLD YOU!
by Lawry's Foods, Inc.
A Special Revised Home Savings Edition — 1977

APPETIZERS
HOT & COLD

Appetizers play a special part in modern cuisine. They make up that added touch of hospitality with festive meals, meant to stimulate but not satisfy. Despite their attractive flavor and appearance and the fact that they appear when appetites are high, appetizers should serve only to introduce the main part of the meal.

A wide variety of appetizers are presented in this chapter, both piping hot and chilled, zesty and mild, for serving with picks or as dips. Each should be carefully garnished to delight the eye as well as the palate. Favorite seasonings such as Seasoned Salt, Seasoned Pepper and Private Blend Lemon Pepper Marinade add that "extra flavor flair."

Bacon Crisps

1 can (10½ oz.) cream of
  mushroom soup
½ teaspoon Lawry's Seasoned
  Pepper

20 thin slices white bread
30 slices (approximately 1 pound)
  wafer-thin bacon, cut in half

Empty the mushroom soup into a small mixing bowl. Add the Seasoned Pepper and blend thoroughly. Trim the crust from the bread. Spread approximately 1 tablespoon of the mushroom soup mixture on each slice of bread. Cut into thirds; place a bread strip on each bacon strip. Roll up and fasten with a wooden pick. Place on a rack in a shallow baking pan or on the broiler tray. Bake in a hot oven (425°F.) for 20 to 30 minutes or until crisp. Makes 5 dozen.

Coconut Chicken Tidbits

2 whole chicken breasts, boned
1½ teaspoons Lawry's Seasoned
  Salt
¼ teaspoon Lawry's Seasoned
  Pepper
½ cup milk
1 egg

½ cup flour
Salad oil
1 package (8 oz.) shredded
  coconut
½ cup chopped chutney
¼ cup butter, melted

Remove the skin from the chicken; cut into 1 inch square pieces. Sprinkle with the Seasoned Salt and Seasoned Pepper. Combine the milk and egg; beat well. Slowly add the flour and continue beating. Dip the chicken pieces in the batter. Roll in the coconut. Fry in deep fat (325°F.) a few at a time, until browned on all sides. (Remove any coconut in the bottom of the pan with a slotted spoon.) Drain on absorbent paper. Combine the chutney and butter. Heat thoroughly. Serve as a dip with the chicken tidbits. Makes about 3 dozen.

Miniature Hungarian Cabbage Rolls

1 large head cabbage
1 egg
½ pound ground beef
¼ pound pork sausage
¼ cup finely chopped onion
¼ cup uncooked rice
¼ cup milk
¾ teaspoon Lawry's Seasoned Salt
¼ teaspoon Lawry's Seasoned Pepper
1 package Lawry's Goulash Seasoning Mix
1 can (1 lb.) tomatoes
1 can (8 oz.) tomato sauce

Separate the cabbage leaves and immerse them in boiling water for about 1 minute until softened. Beat the egg in a bowl. Add the ground beef, pork sausage, onion, rice, milk, Seasoned Salt, Seasoned Pepper, and 1 tablespoon of the Goulash Seasoning Mix. Combine thoroughly with a fork. Blend the remaining Goulash Seasoning Mix, tomatoes, and tomato sauce in a saucepan. Bring to a boil, reduce heat, and simmer for 15 to 20 minutes. Cut the softened cabbage leaves in pieces about 4 x 4 inches, removing the center rib. Place about ½ tablespoon of the meat mixture on each cabbage leaf. Roll up securely. Place in a large, buttered shallow baking dish. Pour the tomato mixture over the cabbage rolls, cover, and bake in a moderate oven (350°F.) for 25 to 30 minutes. Makes about 50.

Creamy Mushrooms

2 cups sliced fresh mushrooms, including stems
¼ teaspoon Lawry's Seasoned Salt
1 cup heavy cream
1 tablespoon Lawry's Garlic Spread
Rye bread rounds

Sprinkle the mushrooms with the Seasoned Salt. Combine all the ingredients except bread in a heavy skillet. Bring to a boil; reduce heat. Simmer, stirring occasionally, until the cream is thick and browned. Place in a chafing dish. Guests serve themselves using the bread rounds as base. Makes about 2½ cups.

Bagna Cauda

2 cans (2 oz. each) anchovy fillets
1 cup butter
½ cup olive oil

2 tablespoons Lawry's Garlic Spread

Drain the anchovies and mince. Combine all the ingredients. Heat 10 minutes; do not boil or brown. Ideal to serve in a fondue pot or a chafing dish as a dip for raw vegetables. Suggested vegetables are: carrot and celery sticks, zucchini spears, red and green cabbage wedges, green pepper strips, cauliflowerettes or raw green beans. To serve, guests dip a vegetable into mixture, using a slice of French bread to catch drippings. This is tradionally served with red wine. Makes about 2 cups.

Hibachi Appetizers

1 package Lawry's Caesar
  Dressing Mix
2 tablespoons water
¼ cup Burgundy or claret
½ cup salad oil

1½ pounds sirloin tip steak,
  cut in 1-inch cubes
Mushroom caps
Cherry tomatoes
Green pepper pieces

Empty the contents of the package into a screw-top, pint-sized jar. Add the water and shake well. Add the wine and oil. Shake again for about 30 seconds. Pour over the cubes of meat and mushroom caps. Marinate for about 2 hours. Arrange the cubes on skewers, alternating with the mushrooms, cherry tomatoes, and green pepper pieces. Grill quickly over charcoal until the meat is nicely browned, for 4 to 6 minutes. Makes about 12 appetizers.

Appetizers

Mock Cheese Shrimp Fondue

1 can (10½ oz.) cream of
   shrimp soup
½ cup milk
2 cups shredded natural Swiss
   cheese

1 tablespoon dry sherry
2 tablespoons Lawry's Garlic
   Spread
2 teaspoons instant minced onion
¼ teaspoon dry mustard

Combine all the ingredients and heat, stirring until the cheese melts and the mixture is thoroughly heated. Makes 2 cups.

Serving suggestion: Ideal to serve in a fondue or chafing dish surrounded with cubes of French bread, along with fondue forks for dunking.

Crunchy Crab Balls

2 cans (6½ oz. each) crabmeat,
   drained and flaked
1 egg, beaten
¾ cup mayonnaise
¼ cup Lawry's Garlic Spread

½ teaspoon dry mustard
⅓ cup minced green pepper
2 tablespoons fine cracker crumbs
Cracker crumbs

Combine the crabmeat, egg, mayonnaise, Garlic Spread, dry mustard, green pepper and 2 tablespoons cracker crumbs. Shape into small balls and roll in the cracker crumbs. (Mixture will be moist until rolled in crumbs.) Fry in deep fat (350°F.) until browned on all sides. Serve warm. Makes about 2½ dozen.

Stuffed Mushroom Caps

24 fresh whole mushrooms
2 tablespoons Lawry's Garlic
Spread
2 tablespoons butter
1 teaspoon Lawry's Seasoned Salt

¼ teaspoon Lawry's Seasoned
Pepper
2 cups fresh bread crumbs
2 tablespoons dry sherry

Wash and drain the mushrooms. Remove the stems, leaving a hollow in the cap which can be stuffed. Melt the Garlic Spread and the butter and blend thoroughly. Dip the caps into the garlic-butter mixture to coat the outside and place on a cooky sheet. Cut the stems into small pieces and saute in the remaining garlic-butter mixture until tender. Add the Seasoned Salt, Seasoned Pepper, and bread crumbs. Toss lightly until well mixed and moisten with the sherry to hold together. Spoon the stuffing into each mushroom cap and bake in a hot oven (425°F.) for 10 minutes. Makes 24 mushrooms.

Delectable Eggplant Dip

1 large eggplant
¼ cup salad oil
¼ cup olive oil
1 clove garlic, peeled
1 large onion, finely chopped
1 green pepper, finely chopped
2 medium tomatoes, peeled
and chopped

2 tablespoons dry sherry
1½ to 2 teaspoons Lawry's
Seasoned Salt
¼ teaspoon Lawry's Seasoned
Pepper

Bake the eggplant in a hot oven (400°F.) about 1 hour or until soft. Remove the skin and chop the pulp. Heat the salad and olive oil with the garlic in a skillet. Saute the onion and green pepper. Remove the garlic. Add the eggplant, tomatoes, sherry, Seasoned Salt and Seasoned Pepper. Cook until thickened, about 15 minutes. Chill thoroughly. Serve with corn or tortilla chips. Makes about 4 cups.

Note: This dip may also be served as a hot or cold relish for meats.

SPICY MEAT LOAVES

2 eggs
1½ pounds ground beef
½ pound ground pork
½ cup finely chopped onions
½ cup bread crumbs

2 teaspoons Lawry's Seasoned Salt
1 package Lawry's Spaghetti Sauce Mix (1½ oz.)
1 can (8 oz.) tomato sauce
1 cup milk

Beat the eggs with a fork. Add the remaining ingredients and mix thoroughly. Pat the meat mixture into a 12x8x2-inch baking dish. Bake in a moderate oven (350°F.) for about 1 hour. Cut meat loaf into thirds lengthwise and slice each third into thick slices. Serve with small Parker house rolls. Makes about 60 sandwiches.

Crispy Chicken Livers

1 pound chicken livers
½ cup flour
2 teaspoons Lawry's Seasoned Salt

2 teaspoons Lawry's Seasoned Pepper
¼ cup butter, melted

Cut each chicken liver into 2 or 3 bite-sized pieces. Mix the flour, Seasoned Salt and Seasoned Pepper. Roll the chicken livers in the seasoned flour. Quickly saute in the melted butter for 3 to 5 minutes. Serve hot with Deviled Dip. Makes 25 to 30 pieces.

Deviled Dip

1 cup dairy sour cream
1 teaspoon Lawry's Seasoned Salt
¼ teaspoon Lawry's Seasoned Pepper
1 tablespoon minced green onion

2 teaspoons prepared mustard
½ cup chopped sweet pickles
1 tablespoon lemon juice
4 to 6 tablespoons light cream

Blend the sour cream, Seasoned Salt, Seasoned Pepper, green onion, mustard, and sweet pickles. Mix thoroughly. Blend in the lemon juice and the cream. Makes about 1½ cups.

Party Pizzas

4 bakery English muffins
1 package Lawry's Spaghetti
  Sauce Mix (1½ oz.)
1 can (1 lb.) tomatoes
1 clove garlic, crushed

½ cup grated Cheddar or
  Parmesan cheese
2 tablespoons minced anchovy
  fillets or 1 pound crumbled
  cooked pork sausage (if desired)

Split the muffins in half, using a fork. Broil to a light brown. Meanwhile, place the Spaghetti Sauce Mix, tomatoes, and crushed garlic in a saucepan. Stir thoroughly. Bring to a boil. Cover and simmer for 20 minutes. Place 2 tablespoons of the sauce on each muffin half. Sprinkle with the cheese and anchovy or the sausage, if desired. Broil until bubbling and brown. Cut each muffin half in 4 wedges and serve hot. Makes 32 pieces. Can be used for 6 English muffins, yielding 48 pieces.

Cocktail Meatballs

1 pound ground beef
½ pound ground pork
1 egg, slightly beaten
1 large onion, grated
1 teaspoon Lawry's Seasoned Salt

¼ teaspoon Lawry's Seasoned
  Pepper
¼ teaspoon allspice
¼ teaspoon cloves
¼ cup flour
½ cup milk

Have the beef and pork ground together (it's best to have the beef ground two extra times). Combine the meat, egg, onion, and seasonings. Add the flour and beat, using an electric mixer, until thoroughly blended and fluffy. Add the milk slowly, 1 tablespoon at a time, beating well. The mixture should be like a thick dough. Shape into small balls. Bake in a shallow baking dish in a moderate oven (375° F.) for about 15 minutes. Serve with prepared spaghetti sauce in a chafing dish. Makes 96 1-inch meatballs.

Note: All beef may be used. For the sauce, prepare Lawry's Spaghetti Sauce Mix with tomato sauce according to the package directions.

Mexican Cheese Ball

2 ounces roasted and peeled
  green chiles (½ of a 4 oz. can)
1 pound sharp Cheddar cheese
1 jar (2 oz.) pimiento, drained
1 tablespoon water

1 package Lawry's Green
  Goddess Salad Dressing Mix
½ cup mayonnaise
¼ cup softened butter

Rinse the seeds from the chiles. Grind the chiles, Cheddar cheese and pimiento, using the medium blade on a food grinder. Blend the water and the Green Goddess Salad Dressing Mix. Add with the mayonnaise and butter to the chiles, cheese and pimiento. Beat with an electric mixer until thoroughly combined. Lightly butter a small mixing bowl. Pack the cheese mixture into the bowl. Cover and refrigerate until firm. Unmold about 30 minutes before serving. Serve with assorted crackers. Makes about 3 cups cheese mixture.

Meatballs Olé

1 package Lawry's Taco Seasoning
  Mix
⅓ cup water

⅓ cup chopped green chiles
1 pound ground beef

Combine Taco Seasoning Mix and water. Add green chiles and ground beef; mix well. Form into 1-inch diameter meatballs. Bake on ungreased jelly roll pan in 350°F. oven 20 minutes. To serve, dip hot meatballs into chilled sauce made with 1 package Lawry's Thousand Island Dressing Mix, 1 tablespoon water and ½ cup catsup. Makes 40 meatballs.

Lemon Pepper Dip

1 pint dairy sour cream	4 teaspoons Lawry's Private Blend Lemon Pepper Marinade

Blend the sour cream and Private Blend Lemon Pepper Marinade. Refrigerate 1 to 2 hours before serving. Serve the dip with assorted raw vegetables. Makes 1 pint dip.

Mushrooms Italiano

1 pound fresh mushrooms	2 tablespoons water
1 package Lawry's Italian Dressing Mix	¼ cup red wine
	⅔ cup salad oil

Rinse the mushrooms well under running water. Remove the stems and drain thoroughly. Prepare Italian dressing following the package directions, using the red wine in place of vinegar. Pour over the mushrooms and allow to marinate for several hours or overnight. Stir occasionally. Serve on cocktail picks. Makes enough marinade for 1 pound mushrooms (20 to 25 medium size).

Walnut Nibblers

3 cups California walnut halves	2 tablespoons Lawry's
1½ tablespoons butter	Seasoned Salt

Spread the nuts in a shallow baking pan. Dot with the butter. Bake in a moderate oven (350° F.) for 20 minutes or until golden brown. When the butter melts, stir the nuts or shake the pan to coat the nuts evenly. Remove from the oven and sprinkle generously with the Seasoned Salt. Spread on absorbent paper to cool. Makes 3 cups.

SPICE 'N SUGAR WALNUTS

1 cup sugar
1 teaspoon Lawry's Seasoned Salt
1 teaspoon cinnamon
½ teaspoon nutmeg

½ teaspoon cloves
½ cup water
2 cups California walnut halves*

Combine the sugar, Seasoned Salt, cinnamon, nutmeg, and cloves in a saucepan. Add the water and stir thoroughly. Bring to a boil and cook to 236° on a candy thermometer (soft ball stage). Remove from heat and add the walnut halves. Stir until the walnuts are well coated. Turn out on waxed paper and separate. Cool and store in a tightly covered container. Makes 2 cups.

*2 cups of pecan halves or toasted whole almonds may be used in place of the walnuts.

Guacamole

2 medium-ripe avocados
1 tablespoon lemon juice
2 medium tomatoes, peeled and
    finely chopped

1 cup finely chopped onion
1½ teaspoons Lawry's Seasoned
    Salt
½ teaspoon Lawry's Seasoned
    Pepper

Mash the avocados with a fork. Add the lemon juice and blend. Add the remaining ingredients and combine thoroughly. Serve with warm tostaditas or king-sized corn chips. Makes about 3 cups.

Garlic Popcorn

3 to 4 tablespoons butter
2 quarts freshly popped corn

1 teaspoon Lawry's Private
    Blend Garlic Salt

Melt the butter and pour over the popped corn. Sprinkle with the Private Blend Garlic Salt. Toss lightly but thoroughly. Serve immediately. Makes 2 quarts.

Chili-Apple Dip

1 tablespoon chopped green pepper	1 package Lawry's Chili Seasoning Mix
⅓ cup sugar	1 apple, finely chopped
⅓ cup wine vinegar	1 package (8 oz.) cream cheese,
⅓ cup chili sauce	softened

Combine all ingredients, except cream cheese, in a sauce pan. Simmer, covered, 30 minutes, stirring occasionally. Whip cream cheese until fluffy. For a mild dip add ⅓ cup chili sauce to cream cheese. For a more flavorful dip add ½ cup chili sauce. Serve with corn chips or fresh vegetables. Remaining sauce can be used as a meat accompaniment, or refrigerated to be used with cream cheese at a later date.

Nuts 'N Bolts

1 cup Wheat Chex	½ cup Spanish peanuts
1 cup Rice Chex	¼ cup butter
1 cup Cheerios	¼ cup salad oil
1 cup thin pretzel sticks	1 teaspoon Lawry's Seasoned Salt

Mix the cereals, pretzel sticks and nuts in a shallow pan. Melt the butter, add the salad oil, and pour over the cereal-nuts mixture. Sprinkle with the Seasoned Salt. Bake in a slow oven (300° F.) for 30 minutes. Stir carefully with a wooden spoon every 10 minutes. Makes 1 quart.

SEASONED
HOT BREADS

One of the most honest and aromatically rewarding experiences in any kitchen is that of baking fresh bread. The wonderful smell, the handsome hot loaf and truly fine eating are all combined in a single undertaking.

It makes little difference if your tastes run to traditional French bread graced with garlic or to convenient refrigerator rolls and biscuits. You will find that such distinctive seasonings as Garlic Spread, Private Blend Garlic Salt and Private Blend Pinch of Herbs can transform even the simplest hot bread recipe into something special to accompany salads, hearty meat dishes or exciting casseroles.

Be creative. Try some of these really unusual hot bread ideas. It promises to be a memorable mealtime experience for the whole family.

Lawry's Garlic Bread

1 loaf French bread
1 jar Lawry's Garlic Spread

½ cup salad oil
Grated Parmesan cheese

Cut the bread in half; then cut each half lengthwise. Score into 5 sections but do not cut through the bottom crust. Melt the Garlic Spread in a shallow pan and add the salad oil. Dip the bread sections into the mixture until they are well saturated. Sprinkle the Parmesan cheese on top. Toast under the broiler until golden brown. Makes 20 slices.

Fancy Garlic Sticks

6 wiener buns
¼ cup Lawry's Garlic Spread
¼ cup butter or margarine

¼ cup grated Parmesan cheese
Poppy seeds and/or sesame seeds

Cut the wiener buns in half lengthwise. Then cut each half lengthwise to make sticks. Melt the Garlic Spread and butter or margarine together and brush the cut sides of the buns. Sprinkle with the grated cheese, poppy and/or sesame seeds. Place on a cooky sheet and toast in a hot oven (450° F.) for about 8 minutes. Serve hot. Makes 24 sticks.

Note: Excellent with green salads and Italian-type casseroles.

Herb Seasoned Bread

3 tablespoons Lawry's Garlic
Spread
3 tablespoons soft butter or
margarine

¼ teaspoon Lawry's Private
Blend Pinch of Herbs
6 slices white bread

Blend the Garlic Spread and butter thoroughly. Add the Private Blend Pinch of Herbs and mix well. Place the bread on a cooky sheet and toast one side under the broiler until light brown. Spread the herb butter on the untoasted side of the bread. Bake in a hot oven (450°F.) for 6 minutes or until golden brown. Cut each slice in half and serve hot. Makes 12 halves.

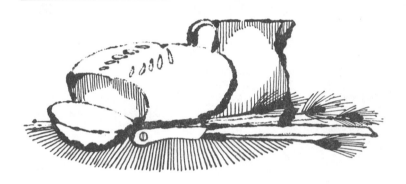

Sesame French Rolls

6 French rolls (sour or sweet
dough)
¼ cup Lawry's Garlic Spread
¼ cup butter or margarine

3 tablespoons grated Parmesan
cheese
2 tablespoons sesame seeds

Cut the French rolls in half lengthwise. Blend the Garlic Spread, butter or margarine, and Parmesan cheese. Spread each roll with the garlic butter mixture. Sprinkle with the sesame seeds. Broil until golden brown. Makes 12.

Note: 6 wiener buns or 6 hamburger buns may be used in place of the French rolls.

Tangy Garlic Strips

2 tablespoons Lawry's Garlic
  Spread
2 tablespoons butter

6 slices white bread
Lawry's Seasoned Pepper
Sesame seeds or dill seed

Melt the Garlic Spread and butter together. Remove the crusts from the bread. Cut each slice into 3 or 4 strips. Brush with the garlic-butter mixture. Sprinkle lightly with the Seasoned Pepper and sesame or dill seed. Bake in very hot oven (450° F.) for 8 to 10 minutes. Makes 6 servings.

Garlic Muffins

4 bakery English muffins
3 tablespoons Lawry's Garlic
  Spread

3 tablespoons butter
Grated Parmesan cheese

Split the muffins in half, using a fork. Toast until slightly browned. Blend the Garlic Spread and butter. Spread each muffin half with the garlic butter. Sprinkle lightly with the grated Parmesan cheese. Broil until golden brown. Makes 8 muffin halves.

Variation: Omit the Parmesan cheese and sprinkle generously with sesame seeds.

Garlic Bread Crumb Topping

½ cup fine bread crumbs
½ teaspoon Lawry's Seasoned Salt

1 tablespoon Lawry's Garlic
  Spread, melted

Mix the bread crumbs and Seasoned Salt. Pour the Garlic Spread over the seasoned crumbs and toss lightly with a fork. Use as a topping for casserole dishes and vegetables. Makes ½ cup.

Garlic Croutons

6 slices white bread
Lawry's Seasoned Salt

¼ cup Lawry's Garlic Spread,
melted

Cut the bread into ¾-inch cubes. Place the bread cubes in a shallow pan. Brown in a slow oven (300° F.) for 30 to 45 minutes. Stir occasionally. While still hot, sprinkle with the Seasoned Salt and stir. Then drizzle the melted Garlic Spread over the bread cubes. Toss gently. Makes 3 to 4 cups.

Note: Use for Caesar-type salads.

Toasted Party Rye Slices

1 loaf sliced party rye bread
  (about 36 slices)
¼ cup butter or margarine

¼ cup Lawry's Garlic Spread
¼ cup grated Parmesan cheese

Toast one side of the rye bread slices under the broiler until light brown. Blend the butter and Garlic Spread thoroughly. Then spread on the untoasted side of the rye bread slices. Sprinkle with the Parmesan cheese. Toast under the broiler. Serve hot. Makes about 36 slices.

Almond Topping

2 tablespoons butter
1 cup fine bread crumbs

1 teaspoon Lawry's Seasoned Salt
½ cup chopped almonds

Melt the butter in a saucepan. Add the bread crumbs and Seasoned Salt, stirring constantly until the crumbs are lightly browned. Add the chopped almonds and continue stirring. Use as a topping for buttered vegetables and for casseroles. Makes 1½ cups.

Patio Pizza Bread

1 package (13¾ oz.) hot roll mix   1 package Lawry's Spaghetti
                                      Sauce Mix (1½ oz.)

Follow the package directions for preparing the rolls except add the
Spaghetti Sauce Mix after the yeast has dissolved. After the dough
rises, shape it into 2 round loaves. Place them in 2 greased 8 or 9 - inch
round pans. Allow the loaves to rise. Bake in a moderate oven (375° F.)
for about 30 minutes. Makes 2 loaves.

Spanish Rice Stuffing

½ cup butter
2 cups chopped onion
2 cups chopped celery
1 package (14 oz. – approximately
  10 cups) prepared poultry
  stuffing

2 packages Lawry's Spanish Rice
  Seasoning Mix
2 cups water

Melt the butter in a large skillet. Add the onions and celery. Cook for
about 5 minutes until crisp-tender. In a large bowl, lightly mix the
prepared poultry stuffing with the onion-celery mixture. Combine the
Spanish Rice Seasoning Mix with the water. Stir thoroughly. Slowly
add this liquid to the stuffing mixture and toss thoroughly. Makes
12 cups, enough for about a 12-pound turkey.

Pepper Bread Sticks

6 wiener buns
½ cup butter or margarine,
  softened

½ teaspoon Lawry's Seasoned
  Pepper
½ teaspoon Lawry's Seasoned Salt
1 cup grated Parmesan cheese

Cut the wiener buns in half lengthwise. Then cut each half lengthwise to make sticks. Blend the butter or margarine and add the Seasoned Pepper and Seasoned Salt. Spread the butter mixture on the bread sticks. Sprinkle with the grated cheese. Place on a cooky sheet and toast in a hot oven (450° F.) for about 8 minutes. Serve hot. Makes 24 sticks.

Note: Especially good with green salads and bland casseroles or vegetable dishes.

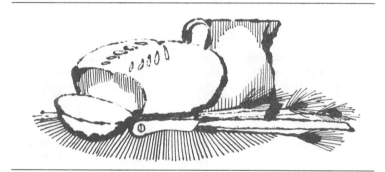

Quick Garlic Bread

½ cup softened butter
2 teaspoons Lawry's Private
  Blend Garlic Salt

1 loaf French bread
  (long and unsliced)

Blend the butter and Private Blend Garlic Salt thoroughly. Allow to stand for a few hours. Cut the bread in half crosswise; then slice each half lengthwise. Score each section into 5 pieces, but do not cut through the bottom crust. Spread the garlic butter on the bread. Toast under the broiler until golden brown. Makes 20 slices.

CASSEROLES
& ENTREES

Casserole cookery is a blessing to many modern homemakers who need to make the most of both budget and kitchen time. It's fun too! Casserole cuisine is also inspired cooking, limited only by the imagination and what's on hand for starters. Perfect for company buffets and easy to do, just a little skill is required to whip up something as simple as Beef & Spaghetti Casserole, or as elegant as Enchiladas Rancheros.

Casseroles also introduce a "change of pace" for dinners and luncheons, offering a wide variety of menu themes. The Enchiladas Rancheros recipe is just one of many new dishes included in "Cooking Secrets Your Mother Never Told You" drawing on the color and flavor of Old Mexico.

Just for fun, read through the recipes in this chapter and see what endless variety is available using seasoned blends and short-cut cooking methods. Then check your casserole collection. You should have several, in a variety of shapes and sizes. Individual ramekins might be the smallest, with a casserole big enough for two nice chickens as the largest.

And don't forget casseroles for entertaining crowds. Many entrees can be prepared and just warmed-up or "finished" in the oven at the last minute. Think casseroles and be a guest at your next party!

24

Chili Cheese Dogs

½ pound ground beef
1 package Lawry's Chili
 Seasoning Mix
1 can (6 oz.) tomato paste
1 cup water

1 can (15½ oz.) kidney beans,
 drained
1 teaspoon prepared mustard
12 frankfurters
12 frankfurter buns
¾ cup grated Cheddar cheese

Brown the ground beef until crumbly; drain fat. Add the Chili Seasoning Mix, tomato paste and water; mix well. Add the kidney beans and mustard; simmer for 10 minutes, stirring frequently. Place the frankfurters in buns, top with ¼ cup of the chili meat sauce and 1 tablespoon of the cheese. Wrap each Chili Cheese Dog securely in aluminum foil. Heat in a hot oven (400°F.) for 15 minutes. Makes 3 cups chili meat sauce — 6 servings.

Dinner-In-One Meat Loaf

1 package Lawry's Meat Loaf
 Seasoning Mix
1½ cups water
2 pounds ground beef

1 can (1 lb.) cut green beans,
 drained or 1 package (9 oz.)
 frozen cut green beans, cooked
 according to package directions
 and drained
3 cups warm mashed potatoes*

Blend the Meat Loaf Seasoning Mix and water in a large bowl. Add the ground beef and combine lightly but thoroughly with a fork. Pat the meat mixture into a 12 x 12-inch square on a piece of wax paper. Spread the green beans to within 1 inch of all edges. Lightly pat into the meat. With the aid of the wax paper roll the meat, jelly-roll fashion. Seal the ends; use the wax paper to transfer to a baking dish. Bake in a moderate oven (375°F.) for 35 minutes. Remove from the oven. Spread the mashed potatoes over the entire meat roll. Return to the oven and bake for an additional 40 minutes. Place the meat roll under the broiler for a few seconds to brown the potatoes, if desired. Allow to stand for about 10 minutes before slicing. Makes 6 to 8 servings.

*Instant mashed potatoes work very nicely for topping.

Pasta Verdura

2 tablespoons olive oil
1 medium onion, thinly sliced
1 package Lawry's Spaghetti
  Sauce Mix (1½ oz.)
1 can (8 oz.) tomato sauce
1½ cups water
4 zucchini
1 small eggplant

1 medium green pepper
3 medium tomatoes
½ cup olive oil
1½ tablespoons Lawry's Seasoned
  Salt
½ pound noodles or spaghetti
¼ pound Mozzarella cheese,
  grated

Heat the 2 tablespoons oil in a skillet and sauté the onion. Add the Spaghetti Sauce Mix, tomato sauce, and water. Bring to a boil, reduce heat, and simmer slowly for about 5 minutes. Cut the unpeeled zucchini in ½-inch crosswise slices. Pare the eggplant, slice thinly, and cut each slice into quarters. Cut the green pepper into 1-inch squares. Cut the tomatoes in small wedges. Heat the ½ cup oil in a second skillet and sauté the zucchini, eggplant, green pepper, and tomatoes. Add the hot spaghetti sauce and Seasoned Salt to the vegetables. Mix carefully and continue to cook over low heat for 20 minutes. Cook the noodles according to the package directions. Drain and butter. When ready to serve, top each serving of noodles with the hot vegetables and sauce. Sprinkle with the grated cheese and serve immediately. Makes 6 servings.

Old Fashioned Chicken and Noodles

8 ounces egg noodles, cooked
and drained
1 cup grated Monterey Jack
cheese
1¼ teaspoons Lawry's Seasoned
Salt
Dash Lawry's Seasoned Pepper

1 package Lawry's Chicken
Gravy Mix
1¼ cups water
1 cup light cream
2 cups cooked, cut up chicken
Chopped parsley

Mix the noodles with all but ¼ cup of the cheese. Add the Seasoned
Salt and Seasoned Pepper. Pour into a buttered 2-quart baking dish.
Blend the Chicken Gravy Mix with water and cream. Bring to a boil;
reduce heat and simmer, uncovered, 5 to 7 minutes, stirring constantly. Combine the chicken and noodles; pour the sauce over the
noodle mixture. Sprinkle with the remaining ¼ cup cheese. Bake in a
moderate oven (375°F.) for about 25 minutes or until browned. Sprinkle with chopped parsley. Makes 6 servings.

Beef Olé

1 pound ground beef
1 package Lawry's Taco
Seasoning Mix
1 can (6 oz.) tomato paste
1½ cups water
1 package (11 oz.) corn chips
Shredded lettuce

Grated cheese
Chopped tomatoes
Sliced ripe olives
Chopped onion
Sliced avocado
Dairy sour cream

Brown the ground beef in a skillet until crumbly. Drain fat. Add the
Taco Seasoning Mix, tomato paste and water. Mix thoroughly. Bring
to a boil, reduce heat and simmer, uncovered, 20 to 25 minutes. Serve
¾ cup of the meat mixture over 1 cup corn chips. Top with the lettuce,
cheese, tomatoes, olives, onion, avocado or sour cream. Makes 3 cups
—serves 4.

Enchiladas con Queso

1 package Lawry's Enchilada
  Sauce Mix
1 can (6 oz.) tomato paste
3 cups water

6 cups grated (about 1½ pounds)
  mild Cheddar or Monterey Jack
  cheese
1 cup finely chopped onion
8 corn tortillas

Empty the contents of the Enchilada Sauce Mix into a 2-quart saucepan. Add the tomato paste and water. Blend thoroughly. Bring to a boil, reduce heat and simmer 15 minutes; stir occasionally. Keep the sauce hot while preparing the enchilada filling. Combine 5 cups of the cheese with the onion. Pour ½ cup of the prepared enchilada sauce into a shallow 13 x 9-inch baking dish. Dip each tortilla into the remaining hot enchilada sauce. Place approximately ½ cup of the cheese mixture in the center of each tortilla. Fold sides over the filling and place in the baking dish, seam side down. Repeat with the remaining tortillas. Pour the remaining sauce over the enchiladas. Sprinkle with 1 cup of the cheese. Bake in a moderate oven (350°F.) for 20 minutes. Makes 4 servings of 2 enchiladas each.

San Francisco Mish Mash

1 pound ground beef
½ cup chopped onion
1 can (4 oz.) sliced mushrooms,
  drained
1 package (10 oz.) frozen
  chopped spinach, thawed

2 teaspoons Lawry's Private Blend
  Garlic Salt
¼ to ½ teaspoon oregano, basil
  or marjoram
4 eggs, beaten

Brown the ground beef until crumbly. Drain off the fat. Add the onions, mushrooms, spinach, Private Blend Garlic Salt, and oregano or basil or marjoram. Cook and stir for about 4 minutes, or until the onions are tender and the spinach is cooked. Add the eggs and cook until the eggs are set. Makes 4 to 5 servings.

Mexican Lasagna

1½ pounds ground beef
1 medium onion, chopped
1 clove garlic, minced
2 cans (1 lb. each) tomatoes
1 package Lawry's Taco
  Seasoning Mix
1 can (4½ oz.) chopped ripe
  olives

1 teaspoon Lawry's Seasoned Salt
¼ cup salad oil
8 corn tortillas
½ pound ricotta cheese
1 egg
½ pound Monterey Jack cheese,
  sliced
½ cup grated Cheddar cheese

Brown the ground beef, onion and garlic in a large skillet until the beef is crumbly. Add the tomatoes, Taco Seasoning Mix, olives and Seasoned Salt. Stir thoroughly. Bring to a boil, reduce heat and simmer 10 minutes. Heat the oil in a small skillet. Dip the tortillas, one at a time, in the hot oil to soften; drain on absorbent paper. Combine the ricotta cheese and egg. Spread ⅓ of the meat mixture in the bottom of a 13 x 9 x 2-inch baking dish. Cover the meat sauce with half of the Monterey Jack cheese and half of the ricotta mixture. Top with a layer of tortillas that have been cut in half. Repeat layers one more time ending with the meat sauce. Sprinkle with the Cheddar cheese. Bake in a moderate oven (350°F.) for 20 minutes. Let stand 5 minutes before cutting. Makes 6 to 8 servings.

Continental Lasagna

½ pound green lasagna noodles,
  spinach flavored*
2 pounds pork sausage
2 cloves garlic, crushed
½ cup chopped onion
1 teaspoon Lawry's Seasoned
  Pepper
1 can (6 oz.) tomato paste
Drained mushroom liquid
¼ cup butter

¼ cup flour
1½ cups milk
½ cup dry white wine, such
  as Chablis
1 teaspoon Lawry's Seasoned Salt
½ cup chopped parsley
1 can (4 oz.) sliced mushrooms
  and liquid
½ pound ricotta cheese
½ cup Parmesan cheese

Boil the lasagna noodles in salted water until almost tender; drain and rinse. Brown the sausage in a large skillet; drain off the fat. Add the garlic, onion, Seasoned Pepper, tomato paste, and mushroom liquid to the sausage. Simmer for 15 minutes. Meanwhile prepare a white sauce: melt the butter in a saucepan and blend in the flour until smooth. Gradually add the milk, stirring constantly until the sauce is smooth and thick. Then stir in the wine, Seasoned Salt, parsley, and mushrooms. Pour ½ cup of the white sauce in a 12x8x2-inch baking dish. Cover the sauce with strips of the lasagna. Spread ½ of the sausage mixture on the lasagna and top with spoonfuls of the ricotta cheese. Pour on ½ of the remaining white sauce. Repeat the layers once again, ending with white sauce, and top with Parmesan cheese. Bake in a moderate oven (350° F.) for 20 minutes. Makes 6 to 8 servings.

*Plain lasagna noodles may be used in place of the green noodles.

Spaghetti Caruso

1 package Lawry's Spaghetti
  Sauce Mix (1½ oz.)
1 can (1 lb. 12 oz.) tomatoes
½ teaspoon Lawry's Seasoned Salt

2 tablespoons butter
½ pound chicken livers, cut
  in half
¼ cup sherry

Place the Spaghetti Sauce Mix, tomatoes, and Seasoned Salt in a saucepan; mix thoroughly. Bring to a boil, reduce heat, cover, and simmer for 20 minutes. Meanwhile sauté the chicken livers in the butter in a skillet over low heat for about 5 minutes. Add the chicken livers and wine to the spaghetti sauce and simmer for 10 minutes. Serve over cooked spaghetti or rice. Makes 4 servings.

Lenten Cabbage Rolls

1 large head cabbage
1 can (8 oz.) mushroom stems
  and pieces, drained
¾ cup uncooked white rice
1 cup chopped onion
1 cup chopped celery
1 egg, slightly beaten

4 teaspoons Lawry's Seasoned Salt
¼ teaspoon Lawry's Seasoned
  Pepper
1 package Lawry's Spaghetti
  Sauce Mix (1½ oz.)
1 can (1 lb. 12 oz.) tomatoes
1 can (8 oz.) tomato sauce

Core the cabbage and parboil for about 10 minutes. Remove 12 large leaves and trim off the thick part. Combine the mushrooms, rice, onion, celery, egg, Seasoned Salt, and Seasoned Pepper. Place about ¼ cup of the mushroom-rice mixture in the cup part of each leaf. Loosely fold over the sides of each leaf; roll up. Place the Spaghetti Sauce Mix in a Dutch oven. Add the tomatoes and tomato sauce; mix thoroughly. Arrange layers of the stuffed cabbage with seam sides down in the sauce. Cover and simmer for 1 hour. Makes 12 rolls, 6 servings.

Peppery Pizza Pie

1 package Lawry's Spaghetti
  Sauce Mix (1½ oz.)
1 can (1 lb.) tomatoes
2 tablespoons salad oil
1 teaspoon Lawry's Seasoned
  Pepper

½ pound Mozzarella cheese,
  sliced thin
Grated Parmesan cheese
Lawry's Seasoned Pepper
1 package hot roll mix

Place the Spaghetti Sauce Mix, tomatoes, oil, and Seasoned Pepper in a small saucepan. Mix thoroughly. Cover and simmer for 25 minutes. Meanwhile, prepare the dough according to the package directions but do not allow to rise. Roll the dough to fit 2 greased 12-inch pizza pans. Brush with oil. Spread the pizza sauce over the dough, top with the cheese slices and sprinkle with the Parmesan cheese and Seasoned Pepper. Bake in a hot oven (400° F.) for about 20 minutes. Cut each pizza into 8 large pieces. Serve at once. Makes 16 servings.

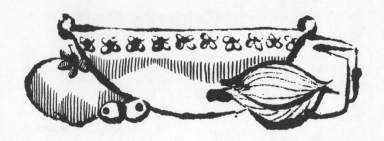

Chiles Rellenos with Spicy Tomato Sauce

1 package Lawry's Taco
  Seasoning Mix
1 can (1 lb.) tomatoes
6 fresh green chiles or 1 can
  (7 oz.) peeled green chiles
¼ pound Monterey Jack or mild
  Cheddar cheese, cut into 6 strips,
  about ½ x ½ x 4 inches

¼ cup flour
½ teaspoon Lawry's Seasoned
  Salt
2 eggs
¼ teaspoon cream of tartar
1 cup salad oil (approximate)

Spicy Tomato Sauce: Combine the Taco Seasoning Mix and tomatoes in a saucepan. Bring to a boil, reduce heat, and simmer for 15 minutes.

If fresh chiles are used, cut off the stem ends and rinse with cold water to remove the seeds. Broil the chiles until the skin browns and blisters. Peel the chiles immediately, while they are still warm. If canned chiles are used, gently rinse with cold water to remove the seeds. Stuff each chile with a strip of cheese. Combine the flour and Seasoned Salt. Separate the egg yolks and whites. Beat the yolks until they are lemon-yellow and slightly thickened. Beat the whites until they are foamy. Add the cream of tartar and continue beating until the whites hold a stiff peak. Carefully fold the yolks into the whites. Heat the oil in a skillet. Roll the stuffed chiles in the seasoned flour. Dip into the egg batter. Fry in the hot oil on each side until golden brown. Drain on absorbent paper. Serve immediately with Spicy Tomato Sauce. Makes 6.

Spicy Beef Boats

1 package Lawry's Goulash
  Seasoning Mix
½ cup water
1 pound ground beef
¼ cup finely chopped celery

1 cup grated Cheddar cheese
6 large or 12 small French rolls
¼ cup butter, melted
1 teaspoon Lawry's Private Blend
  Garlic Salt

Combine the Goulash Seasoning Mix and water in a bowl. Add the ground beef, celery, and ½ cup of the cheese. Hollow out the French rolls, being careful not to break the crust. Combine the butter and Private Blend Garlic Salt. Brush butter mixture on the outside of the rolls. Fill the rolls with the meat mixture. Sprinkle with the remaining ½ cup of cheese. Place on a cooky sheet. Bake in a slow oven (325°F.) for 45 minutes. Makes 6 servings.

Spareribs & Kraut Caraway

1 tablespoon salad oil
3 pounds spareribs, cut in serving
  size pieces
2 teaspoons Lawry's Seasoned
  Salt
1 package Lawry's Beef Stew
  Seasoning Mix

1 can (1 lb. 11 oz.) sauerkraut
1 tart apple, pared and chopped
1 can (8 oz.) tomato sauce
½ cup water
2 tablespoons brown sugar
2 teaspoons caraway seeds

Heat the oil in a Dutch oven. Sprinkle the spareribs with the Seasoned Salt. Brown thoroughly on all sides. Pour off the fat. Combine the remaining ingredients. Pour over the spareribs. Cover and simmer 1½ hours, basting with the juices several times during cooking. Skim off the excess fat while cooking and again before serving. Makes 4 to 6 servings.

Baked Sour Cream Tacos

½ cup chopped onion
2 tablespoons salad oil
1 can (1 lb. 12 oz.) tomatoes
1 package Lawry's Spanish Rice
Seasoning Mix
2 tablespoons Salsa Jalapeña
12 tortillas

½ cup salad oil
1 pound Monterey Jack cheese,
grated
¾ cup chopped onion
1 pint dairy sour cream
1 teaspoon Lawry's Seasoned Salt
Lawry's Seasoned Pepper

Sauté the ½ cup onion in the 2 tablespoons salad oil until tender. Add the tomatoes, Spanish Rice Seasoning Mix, and Salsa Jalapena. Simmer for 15 to 20 minutes; set aside to cool. Fry the tortillas lightly in the ½ cup oil for 10 to 15 seconds on each side. Do not let them get crisp. Put about 2 tablespoons of the cheese, 1 tablespoon of the onion, and 2 tablespoons of the sauce on each tortilla. Roll the tortillas and place them seam side down, forming a single layer, in a large, shallow buttered baking dish. Pour the remaining sauce over the top of the rolled tortillas and sprinkle any remaining cheese over the sauce. Combine the sour cream and Seasoned Salt and spoon it over the tortillas. Sprinkle lightly with the Seasoned Pepper. Bake in a slow oven (325° F.) for 25 to 30 minutes. Makes 6 to 12 servings.

Sloppy Joes with Beans

½ pound ground beef
1 package Lawry's Sloppy Joe
Seasoning Mix
1 cup water

1 can (6 oz.) tomato paste
1 can (1 lb.) kidney or pinto
beans

Brown the ground beef until crumbly. Drain the fat. Add the Sloppy Joe Seasoning Mix, water, tomato paste, and kidney or pinto beans. Stir thoroughly. Bring to a boil, reduce heat, and simmer for 10 minutes. Delicious over buns, frankfurters, or hamburgers. Makes 6 to 8 servings.

Chilaquiles

1 medium onion, chopped
2 tablespoons salad or olive oil
1 can (1 lb. 12 oz.) tomatoes
1 package Lawry's Spanish Rice
Seasoning Mix
½ teaspoon Lawry's Seasoned
Salt

1 can (4 oz.) peeled green chiles,
seeds removed and chopped
1 package (6¼ oz.) tortilla chips
¾ pound Monterey Jack cheese,
sliced or grated
1 cup dairy sour cream
½ cup grated Cheddar cheese

To make sauce: Sauté the onion in the 2 tablespoons salad or olive oil until tender. Add the tomatoes, Spanish Rice Seasoning Mix, Seasoned Salt and chopped green chiles. Simmer for 10 to 15 minutes. In a buttered 2-quart casserole, layer ½ of the tortilla chips, sauce and Monterey Jack cheese. Repeat the layers. Top with the sour cream. Bake in a slow oven (325°F.) for 30 minutes. Sprinkle with the Cheddar cheese and bake for 10 minutes longer. Let stand 15 minutes before serving. Makes 6 to 8 servings.

CHILI CHIP CASSEROLE

1 pound ground beef
1 cup chopped onion
  (1 medium onion)
1 package Lawry's Chili
  Seasoning Mix
1 can (6 oz.) tomato paste

¾ cup water
1 bag (6 oz.) corn chips
1 can (1 lb.) pinto beans
2 cans (2¼ oz. each) sliced
  ripe olives
2 cups grated Cheddar cheese

Brown the ground beef until crumbly; drain fat. Add the onion, Chili Seasoning Mix, tomato paste, and water. Combine thoroughly. Simmer for about 10 minutes. Place ½ bag (about 2 cups) of the corn chips in the bottom of a 2-quart casserole. Spoon ½ of the chili-meat mixture over the corn chips. Place ½ of the can of pinto beans over the meat mixture. Then place 1 can of the olives over the beans. Sprinkle with 1 cup of the grated cheese. Repeat the meat, pinto bean and olive layers. Then arrange the remaining corn chips over the top and sprinkle with the remaining cup of grated cheese. Cover and bake in a moderate oven (350°F.) for 30 minutes. Uncover and bake for an additional 15 minutes. Makes 6 to 8 servings.

California Tamale Pie

¾ cup yellow corn meal
1½ cups milk
1 egg, beaten
1 pound lean ground beef
1 package Lawry's Chili
  Seasoning Mix
2 teaspoons Lawry's Seasoned Salt

1 can (1 lb.) tomatoes
1 can (17 oz.) whole-kernel corn,
  drained
1 can (7½ oz.) ripe olives,
  drained
1 cup grated Cheddar cheese

Mix the corn meal, milk, and egg in a 2½-quart casserole. Brown the meat in a skillet until crumbly. Add the Chili Seasoning Mix, Seasoned Salt, tomatoes, corn, and olives; mix well. Stir into the corn meal mixture. Bake in a moderate oven (350° F.) for 1 hour and 15 minutes. Sprinkle the grated cheese on top and bake until the cheese melts, about 5 minutes longer. Makes 6 to 8 servings.

Tortilla Casserole

12 tortillas, cut in eighths
½ cup salad oil
Lawry's Seasoned Salt
1 medium onion, chopped
2 tablespoons salad or olive oil
1 can (1 lb. 12 oz.) tomatoes
1 package Lawry's Chili
  Seasoning Mix

½ teaspoon Lawry's Seasoned
  Salt
½ cup grated Parmesan cheese
8 ounces Monterey Jack cheese,
  sliced
1 pint dairy sour cream
½ cup grated Cheddar cheese

Fry the tortillas in the ½ cup hot salad oil until crisp. Drain on absorbent paper and sprinkle lightly with Seasoned Salt. To make the sauce: sauté the onion in the 2 tablespoons salad or olive oil until tender. Add the tomatoes, Chili Seasoning Mix and Seasoned Salt. Simmer for 10 to 15 minutes. In a buttered 2-quart casserole layer ½ of the tortilla chips, sauce, Parmesan cheese, Monterey Jack cheese and sour cream. Repeat, ending with the sour cream. Bake in a slow oven (325°F.) for 30 minutes. Sprinkle with additional Cheddar cheese and bake for 10 minutes longer. Makes 6 to 8 servings.

Taco Pizza

1 pound ground beef
1 package Lawry's Taco
  Seasoning Mix
1 cup water

1 package (13¼ oz.) hot roll mix
Salad oil, as needed
1 can (8 oz.) tomato sauce
2 cups grated Cheddar cheese

Brown the ground beef until crumbly; drain fat. Add the Taco Seasoning Mix and water; stir. Bring to a boil. Reduce heat and simmer for 15 to 20 minutes, stirring occasionally. Meanwhile, prepare the dough according to the package directions, but do not allow to rise. Roll the dough to fit a greased 16½x12-inch baking sheet. Brush with oil. Spread the taco meat over dough. Then spread the tomato sauce over meat. Top with the cheese. Bake in a hot oven (400°F.) on bottom shelf for 15 to 20 minutes. Cut in squares. Makes 4 servings.

BARBECUED BEEF ON TOASTED BUNS

2 teaspoons Lawry's Seasoned Salt	1 can (8 oz.) tomato sauce
2½ to 3 pounds boned chuck pot roast	1 teaspoon brown sugar
2 cups water	⅛ teaspoon liquid smoke
1 package Lawry's Beef Stew Seasoning Mix	8 to 10 hamburger buns, toasted

Rub the Seasoned Salt on the pot roast. Place the water and pot roast in a Dutch oven. Cover and simmer for 2 to 2½ hours or until the meat is very tender. Remove the meat; allow it to cool while making a sauce. Use 2 cups of the meat juices in the Dutch oven. Add the Beef Stew Seasoning Mix, tomato sauce, brown sugar, and liquid smoke. Mix thoroughly. Simmer for 20 minutes. Shred the meat with a sharp knife and add to the sauce. Blend well and heat thoroughly. Spoon on the toasted hamburger buns. Makes 8 to 10 servings.

Magyar Eggplant

1 medium eggplant	1 package Lawry's Goulash Seasoning Mix
2 eggs, beaten	
¾ to 1 cup dry bread crumbs	1¾ cups water
½ to 1 cup salad or olive oil	½ cup Parmesan cheese

Peel the eggplant and cut in slices ¼ inch thick. Dip the slices in the beaten eggs, then in the bread crumbs. Pour a small amount of the oil in a skillet and heat. Quickly saute the eggplant slices, adding a little of the oil at a time. (Discard the brown crumbs that may collect in the skillet; wipe the skillet with paper toweling.) Combine the Goulash Seasoning Mix and water. Stir thoroughly. Bring to a boil, reduce heat, and simmer for about 10 minutes. In a greased, 1½-quart casserole, place ⅓ of the sliced eggplant. Pour ⅓ of the sauce over the eggplant. Sprinkle with ⅓ of the cheese. Repeat the layers 2 more times. Bake in a moderate oven (350°F.) for about 30 minutes. Makes 4 to 6 servings.

Enchiladas Rancheros

1 package Lawry's Enchilada
  Sauce Mix
1 can (6 oz.) tomato paste
3 cups water
8 fresh green chiles or
  1 can (7 oz.) peeled green chiles

½ pound Monterey Jack or
  mild Cheddar cheese
8 corn tortillas
½ cup dairy sour cream
Lawry's Seasoned Salt

Combine the Enchilada Sauce Mix, tomato paste and water in a saucepan. Bring to a boil, reduce heat and simmer 15 minutes. If fresh chiles are used, cut off the stem ends and rinse with cold water to remove the seeds. Broil the chiles until the skin browns and blisters. Peel the chiles while still warm. If canned chiles are used, gently rinse with cold water to remove the seeds. Cut 8 strips of the cheese, about ½ x ½ x 4 inches. Grate the remaining cheese and reserve. Stuff each chile with a strip of cheese. Dip each tortilla in the hot sauce, then roll one tortilla around each stuffed chile. Place the enchiladas in a 13 x 9-inch baking dish, seam side down. Pour the remaining sauce over the enchiladas and sprinkle with the reserved grated cheese. Bake in a moderate oven (350°F.) for 15 to 20 minutes. Top with the sour cream and sprinkle with the Seasoned Salt. Makes 4 servings of 2 enchiladas each.

TIJUANA TORTE

1 pound ground beef	1 package Lawry's Taco Seasoning
1 medium onion, chopped	Mix
1 can (1 lb.) stewed tomatoes	12 corn tortillas
1 can (8 oz.) tomato sauce	1 pound Cheddar cheese, grated
1 can (4 oz.) chopped green chiles (optional)	

Brown the ground beef and onion in a skillet. Drain the fat.
Add the stewed tomatoes, tomato sauce, green chiles and Taco
Seasoning Mix. Combine thoroughly and simmer 10 to 15 minutes. Place about ¼ cup of the meat mixture in the bottom of a
9 x 13-inch baking dish. Place two tortillas side by side on the
meat mixture. Top each tortilla with some meat mixture and
grated cheese. Repeat until each stack contains 6 tortillas layered
with meat and cheese. Bake in a moderate oven (350°F.) for
20 to 25 minutes or until cheese is bubbly. Cut each torte (stack)
into quarters with a sharp knife before serving. Makes 4 to 6
servings.

Sloppy Joe Casserole

1 pound ground beef	1 can (6 oz.) tomato paste
1 package Lawry's Sloppy Joe Seasoning Mix	1 can (12 oz.) Mexicorn
	8 ounces spiral macaroni
1½ cups water	1 cup grated Cheddar cheese

Brown the ground beef until crumbly. Drain the fat. Add the
Sloppy Joe Seasoning Mix, water, tomato paste, and Mexicorn.
Stir thoroughly. Bring to a boil, reduce heat, and simmer for 5
minutes. Meanwhile, cook the macaroni according to package
directions. Drain and rinse with cold water. Combine the macaroni and meat mixture. Pour into a buttered 2-quart casserole.
Sprinkle with the cheese. Bake in a moderate oven (350°F.) for
25 to 30 minutes. Makes 6 servings.

Mexican Fried Rice

1 cup uncooked rice	1 package Lawry's Spanish Rice
2 tablespoons salad oil	Seasoning Mix
1¾ cups water	

Sauté the rice in the oil until golden. Add the water and Spanish Rice Seasoning Mix. Combine thoroughly. Bring to a boil; reduce heat, cover and simmer slowly 25 to 30 minutes. Makes 4 to 6 servings.

Lasagna

1 pound ground beef	1 package Lawry's Spaghetti
2 teaspoons Lawry's Seasoned Salt	Sauce Mix (1½ oz.)
2 cloves garlic, crushed	½ pound lasagna (broad noodles)
½ teaspoon Lawry's Seasoned	½ pound Mozzarella cheese,
Pepper	sliced
1 can (1 lb. 12 oz.) tomatoes	½ pound ricotta cheese*
1 can (8 oz.) tomato sauce	½ cup Parmesan cheese

Brown the meat in a Dutch oven or deep kettle. Add the Seasoned Salt. Add the crushed garlic and Seasoned Pepper. Simmer slowly for about 10 minutes. Add the canned tomatoes, tomato sauce, and Spaghetti Sauce Mix. Stir thoroughly; cover and simmer for 30 minutes. Meanwhile, boil the lasagna noodles in salted water until they are almost tender; drain and rinse. Pour ¼ of the meat sauce into a 12x8x2-inch baking dish. Cover the meat sauce with ⅓ of the cooked lasagna noodles. Arrange ⅓ of the Mozzarella cheese and ⅓ of the ricotta over the lasagna. Repeat the layers 2 more times, ending with meat sauce, and top with Parmesan cheese. Bake in a moderate oven (350° F.) for 20 minutes. Makes 6 to 8 servings.

*Cottage cheese may be substituted for the ricotta; however, drain thoroughly. To freeze: Prepare as above, except for baking. Cover securely and seal with freezer tape. When ready to use, thaw, remove cover, and bake as directed.

Creamy Turkey Casserole

1 package Lawry's Stroganoff
  Sauce Mix
1½ cups water
½ cup dairy sour cream
4 cups leftover diced turkey*
1 package (8 oz.) bow tie
  macaroni or other macaroni
  product

1 package (10 oz.) frozen peas
  or green beans
1 can (2¼ oz.) sliced ripe
  olives, drained
Sliced almonds, buttered bread
  crumbs, or grated cheese,
  optional

Combine the Stroganoff Sauce Mix and water in a saucepan. Stir thoroughly. Bring to a boil, reduce heat, cover, and simmer for 10 minutes. Meanwhile, cook both macaroni and peas according to package directions. Blend the sour cream into the stroganoff sauce. Add the turkey and mix gently to combine. Remove from heat. In a buttered 2-quart casserole layer ½ of the macaroni, ½ of the peas, ½ of the turkey-and-sauce mixture, and ½ of the olives. Repeat the layers. Top with the sliced almonds, buttered bread crumbs, or grated cheese, if desired. Bake in a slow oven (325°F.) for 30 minutes. Makes 6 to 8 servings.

*Chicken may be used in place of turkey.

Special Fried Burritos

1 can (1 lb. 4 oz.) refried beans
1 package Lawry's Enchilada
  Sauce Mix
¼ cup water

2 tablespoons salad oil
5 flour tortillas
1¼ cups grated American cheese
¼ cup chopped onion

Combine the refried beans, Enchilada Sauce Mix and water in a saucepan. Bring to a boil, reduce heat and simmer for 5 to 10 minutes. Heat the oil in a small skillet. Place about ½ cup of the bean mixture in the center of each tortilla. Sprinkle the cheese and onion over the beans. Fold in opposite edges of each tortilla and roll up to form a package. Fry in hot oil until golden brown. Makes 5 burritos.

Macaroni and Frankfurter Casserole

1 package Lawry's Spaghetti Sauce Mix (1½ oz.)	8 ounces elbow macaroni 6 frankfurters
1 can (1 lb. 12 oz.) tomatoes	½ cup grated American cheese
2 tablespoons salad oil	

Blend the Spaghetti Sauce Mix, tomatoes, and oil in a saucepan. Bring to a boil. Cover and simmer for 20 minutes. Meanwhile cook the macaroni in boiling salted water until tender. Drain and rinse. Slice the frankfurters diagonally into ½-inch pieces. Mix the sauce, macaroni, and frankfurters. Place in a 2-quart casserole. Sprinkle the grated cheese over the top. Bake in a moderate oven (350° F.) for about 30 minutes. Makes 6 servings.

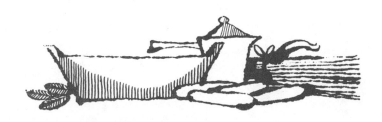

Beef and Spaghetti Casserole

1 pound ground beef	2 cups water
1½ teaspoons Lawry's Seasoned Salt	3 cups cooked spaghetti (8 oz. uncooked)
1 package Lawry's Spaghetti Sauce Mix (1½ oz.)	½ cup grated American cheese Olives, optional
2 cans (8 oz. each) tomato sauce	Green pepper rings, optional

Brown the ground beef in a skillet until crumbly. Drain fat. Add the Seasoned Salt, Spaghetti Sauce Mix, tomato sauce and water. Mix thoroughly. Cover and simmer for 25 minutes. Combine the meat sauce and cooked spaghetti. Place in a 2-quart casserole. Cover and bake in a moderate oven (350°F.) for 15 to 20 minutes. Sprinkle the grated cheese over the spaghetti and place under the broiler to melt the cheese. Top the cheese with olives and green pepper rings, if desired. Makes 4 to 6 servings.

CHEESE & EGGS

Cheese and eggs are perfect flavor partners, appetizing in appearance and versatile in preparation. As a budget stretcher, cheese and eggs offer the perfect high protein substitute for meat dishes. Use them together or separately, in a baked loaf, pudding, casserole, salad or open-face sandwich.

Cheeses offer a world of variety in both taste and national origin. The best way to learn about cheese is to taste it. Most cheeses keep well in the refrigerator, wrapped as airtight as possible. The flavor is usually enhanced if cheeses are served at room temperature.

The secret of good egg cookery is "slow and gentle" handling. Hard-cooked eggs should be simmered gently for 15 minutes to prevent them from becoming tough and rubbery. They should peel easily if cooled quickly under cold running water.

Light flavor distinguishes cheese and egg cookery and such seasonings as Garlic Spread, Private Blend Garlic Salt, Seasoned Salt and Seasoned Pepper are perfect complements.

Fettucine

8 ounces fine noodles
¼ cup butter
¼ cup Lawry's Garlic Spread
½ cup light cream

½ cup grated Parmesan or
Romano cheese
2 tablespoons chopped parsley,
optional

Cook the noodles according to the package directions. Melt the butter and Garlic Spread together slowly. Add the melted butter-Garlic Spread mixture, cream, and grated cheese to the drained hot noodles. Toss lightly. Serve with a light sprinkle of grated cheese and garnish with chopped parsley, if desired. Makes 4 servings.

Baked Eggs and Cheese Pudding

4 slices of bread
2 tablespoons Lawry's Garlic
Spread
4 egg yolks
2 cups milk

1½ teaspoons Lawry's Seasoned
Salt
1 cup grated sharp Cheddar cheese
¼ cup sliced stuffed olives
4 egg whites

Spread each slice of bread with 1½ teaspoons of the Garlic Spread. Cut the bread into 1-inch cubes. Beat the egg yolks, milk, and Seasoned Salt in a large mixing bowl until foamy. Add the bread cubes, cheese, and olives. Mix thoroughly. Beat the egg whites until stiff and fold into the bread and egg mixture. Pour into an ungreased, 2-quart casserole. Bake in a slow oven (325° F.) for 50 to 60 minutes or until a knife comes out clean. Makes 6 servings.

Scotch Rarebit

2 tablespoons butter
1 pound Cheddar cheese, cubed
1 teaspoon Lawry's Seasoned Salt
½ teaspoon dry mustard

Small pinch cayenne pepper
1 teaspoon Worcestershire sauce
½ cup milk
2 eggs, slightly beaten

Melt the butter in the top of a double boiler. Add the cheese and stir until it is melted. Add the Seasoned Salt, mustard, cayenne, Worcestershire sauce, and milk. Add the eggs gradually, stirring constantly to prevent curdling. Cook, stirring constantly, until it thickens. Serve with cubes of French bread or over toast points. Makes 4 servings.

Puffed Eggs Monterey

6 eggs
½ cup milk
1 teaspoon Lawry's Seasoned Salt
½ teaspoon Lawry's Seasoned Pepper

2 tablespoons chopped green chiles
¾ cup grated Monterey Jack cheese
4 slices white bread
2 tablespoons butter

Combine the eggs, milk, Seasoned Salt, Seasoned Pepper and chiles; beat lightly. Add the cheese. Spread the bread with butter; cut in half to make triangles. Arrange the bread halves, buttered side out, around edge of a 9-inch pie plate so points stand up. Place remaining bread, buttered side down in bottom of pan. Pour in egg mixture. Bake in a 350°F. oven for 30 minutes. Cut into wedges. Makes 6 servings.

Pickled Eggs

¾ cup beet juice
¾ cup red wine vinegar
½ cup rosé wine
1 bay leaf
¼ teaspoon allspice

2 teaspoons Lawry's Seasoned Salt
½ teaspoon Lawry's Seasoned
Pepper
6 hard-cooked eggs, shelled

Combine all the ingredients except the eggs. Heat for 10 minutes, but do not boil. Pour into a quart jar. Add the eggs. Cover and refrigerate overnight. To serve, cut in halves or quarters. Makes 6 servings.

Eggs Bengal

⅓ cup butter
2 teaspoons curry powder
¼ teaspoon Lawry's Private
Blend Garlic Salt
¼ cup finely chopped onion
½ cup raisins
1 package Lawry's Chicken
Gravy Mix

2½ cups light cream
2 teaspoons lemon juice
¼ teaspoon grated lemon peel
5 hard-cooked eggs, shelled
2 English muffins, halved
4 slices Canadian bacon, cooked

Heat the butter, curry powder and Private Blend Garlic Salt until bubbly. Add the onion; sauté. Stir in the raisins. Blend in the Chicken Gravy Mix and light cream. Bring to a boil, reduce heat and simmer 5 to 7 minutes, stirring constantly. Add the lemon juice and lemon peel; blend well. Halve 4 of the hard-cooked eggs and chop the remaining egg. Toast and butter the English muffin halves. To serve: place a slice of cooked Canadian bacon on each muffin half. Top with 2 egg halves. Spoon the sauce over the eggs. Sprinkle the top with chopped egg. Makes 4 servings.

Cheesy Manicotti Casserole

12 manicotti shells
1 package Lawry's Spaghetti
Sauce Mix (1½ oz.)
1 can (6 oz.) tomato paste
3 cups water
8 ounces ricotta cheese
½ cup Parmesan cheese

8 ounces Mozzarella cheese, grated
2 eggs, beaten
½ cup finely chopped parsley
1 teaspoon Lawry's Seasoned Salt
½ teaspoon Lawry's Seasoned
Pepper

Cook the manicotti shells in salted boiling water for 3 minutes. Drain and allow to cool. Place the Spaghetti Sauce Mix, tomato paste, and the 3 cups water in a 2-quart saucepan. Stir thoroughly. Bring to a boil, reduce heat, and simmer for 10 minutes. Meanwhile, mix the ricotta, Parmesan, and Mozzarella cheeses lightly with a fork reserving 1 cup of the grated Mozzarella for topping. Add the eggs, parsley, Seasoned Salt, and Seasoned Pepper. Mix lightly. Lightly stuff the manicotti shells. Pour 2 cups of the cooked sauce into a 13 x 9 x 2-inch baking dish. Arrange the manicotti shells on the sauce. Pour the remaining sauce over the top. Sprinkle with the reserved 1 cup of Mozzarella cheese. Cover and bake in a moderate oven (350° F.) for 30 minutes. Makes 6 servings.

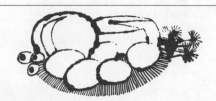

Cheese and Olive Casserole

1 package Lawry's Spanish Rice
Seasoning Mix
3 cups water
2 tablespoons salad oil

1 cup uncooked rice
½ cup sliced ripe olives, drained
1⅓ cups cubed Cheddar cheese

Empty the contents of the package into a 3-quart saucepan. Add the water and salad oil. Mix thoroughly. Bring to a boil. Stir in the rice. Cover and simmer for 25 minutes. Add the sliced olives and cubed cheese. Mix lightly. Place in a greased 1½-quart casserole. Bake in a moderate oven (350° F.) for 15 minutes. Makes 5 to 6 servings.

Chili Cheese Jubilee

2 tablespoons butter
1 medium onion, chopped
1 can (8 oz.) tomato sauce
1 package Lawry's Chili
    Seasoning Mix
½ cup water
2 eggs

1 cup light cream
1 package (6 oz.) corn chips
8 ounces Monterey Jack cheese,
    cubed
1 cup dairy sour cream
½ cup grated Cheddar cheese

Melt the butter in a skillet. Add the onion and sauté until just tender. Add the tomato sauce, Chili Seasoning Mix, and water. Simmer for 5 minutes. Beat the eggs slightly, add the light cream, and mix well. Remove the tomato-chili mixture from heat. Add the egg-cream mixture slowly, stirring constantly. Place ½ of the package of corn chips in the bottom of a 1½-quart casserole. Then add a layer of ½ of the Monterey Jack cheese. Cover with ½ of the sauce. Repeat the layers. Top with the sour cream and sprinkle with the grated Cheddar cheese. Bake in a slow oven (325° F.) for 25 to 30 minutes. Makes 5 to 6 servings.

Eggs a la Goldenrod

3 tablespoons butter
3 tablespoons flour
½ teaspoon Lawry's Seasoned
    Salt

¼ teaspoon Lawry's Seasoned
    Pepper
2 cups milk
6 hard-cooked eggs

Melt the butter in a saucepan. Blend in the flour, Seasoned Salt, and Seasoned Pepper. Cook over low heat until the mixture is smooth and bubbly. Remove from heat. Stir in the milk. Bring to a boil, stirring constantly. Boil one minute. Dice the hard-cooked eggs in large pieces reserving two yolks. Carefully fold the diced eggs into the cream sauce. Press the two yolks through a sieve. Serve the creamed eggs in toast cups.* Garnish with the sieved egg yolk and the Seasoned Pepper. Serve with crisp bacon or link sausages and spiced crab apples. Makes 4 to 6 servings.

*Toast cups: Brush thinly sliced bread (crusts removed) with melted butter. Press into custard cups or muffin tins. Toast in moderate oven (350°F.) for 15 minutes until golden brown.

Eggs El Dorado

1 package Lawry's Taco
  Seasoning Mix
1 can (1 lb.) whole tomatoes
1 large green bell pepper, seeded
  and cut in 1 x ¼ inch strips
2 cans (4 oz. each) mushroom
  stems and pieces, drained
1 package (8 oz.) refrigerator
  crescent rolls

1 cup grated Cheddar cheese
8 eggs, beaten
1 cup dairy sour cream
1 teaspoon salt
Pepper (to taste)
Poppy seeds
Butter

In a "burner to oven" casserole (approximately 2 to 3 quarts) combine the Taco Seasoning Mix, tomatoes, bell pepper and mushrooms. Cover and simmer 10 minutes. Remove the rolls from package and separate into 4 rectangles. (Do not separate into triangles.) Sprinkle each rectangle with ¼ of the cheese. Roll up tightly, jelly roll fashion, and slice each roll into 3 spirals. Combine the eggs, sour cream, salt, and pepper. Remove the tomato mixture from heat. Carefully spoon the egg mixture over it while it is still hot. Place the 12 biscuit spirals on the egg mixture and sprinkle each with poppy seeds. Top each biscuit spiral with a paper thin slice of butter. Bake the casserole in a moderate oven (350°F.) for 30 to 60 minutes or until the biscuits brown and the egg mixture is firm. Makes 6 servings.

Egg Sandwich Filling

4 hard-cooked eggs
½ cup finely chopped celery
2 tablespoons chopped green
  onions
2 tablespoons sweet pickle relish

1 teaspoon Lawry's Seasoned Salt
¼ teaspoon Lawry's Seasoned
  Pepper
¼ cup mayonnaise or salad
  dressing

Chop the hard-cooked eggs and place them in a small mixing bowl. Add the remaining ingredients and mix thoroughly. Refrigerate for several hours. Serve on open-faced sandwiches, in regular sandwiches, or as a canapé spread. Makes 1½ cups.

FISH

Seafood, once enjoyed exclusively in coastal regions, now is available to everyone, thanks to modern canning and freezing. Whether salt-water or fresh-water varieties, fish can make a handsome main dish, served whole or in fillets and garnished with a delicate sauce. It adds nutritious variety to salads, soups and even spaghetti sauce.

Fresh fish is generally preferable to frozen if it is going to be cooked whole. And all seafood should be cooked only until done for best appearance and flavor. Fish is done the moment it flakes easily with a fork.

The light flavor of seafood makes it perfect for seasoning with Spaghetti Sauce Mix and Spanish Rice Seasoning Mix. For an imaginative approach to your next seafood meal, try Shrimp Risotto, Pescada a la Mexicana or the popular Party Paella Valenciana.

Shrimp al Ajillo

2 pounds raw jumbo shrimp,
   in the shell
½ cup butter

¼ cup fresh lemon juice
2 teaspoons Lawry's Private
   Blend Garlic Salt

Shell and devein the shrimp, leaving on the tails. Rinse and drain. Melt the butter in a sauce pan and add lemon juice and Private Blend Garlic Salt. Combine thoroughly. Arrange the shrimp on a broiler pan (without rack) or a heatproof platter. Brush or spoon about half of the butter mixture on the shrimp. Broil 5 to 6 inches from heat for 3 to 4 minutes. Turn and brush with the remaining butter mixture. Broil 3 to 4 minutes longer or until cooked through. (Do not overcook.) Serve immediately with pan juices. Makes 5 servings or about 25 shrimp.

Shrimp Curry

¼ cup butter
½ cup finely chopped onions
2 tablespoons flour
1 teaspoon Lawry's Seasoned Salt
1 teaspoon curry powder

¼ teaspoon Lawry's Seasoned
   Pepper
2 cups milk
2 cups cooked fresh shrimp

Melt the butter in a 2-quart saucepan. Add the onions and sauté for about 5 minutes. Blend in the flour, Seasoned Salt, curry powder, and Seasoned Pepper. Slowly add the milk, stirring constantly. Bring to a boil, reduce heat, and simmer gently for about 10 minutes, stirring occasionally. Add the shrimp and simmer for about 5 minutes more. Serve over fluffy rice. Makes 4 to 6 servings.

Note: For an East Indian dinner, serve the shrimp curry with a selection of the following accompaniments: chopped hard-cooked egg, toasted coconut, crisp bacon bits, mandarin oranges, chutney, raisins, almonds or peanuts.

Fish

Pescada a la Mexicana

1 large onion, chopped	1 teaspoon Lawry's Seasoned
2 tablespoons olive oil	Pepper
1 can (1 lb.) tomatoes	2 pounds fish fillets, such as
1 package Lawry's Spanish Rice	halibut or sole
Seasoning Mix	1 jar (2 oz.) chopped pimientos
1 teaspoon Lawry's Seasoned Salt	1 jar (3 oz.) stuffed green olives

Sauté the onion in the oil until tender. Add the tomatoes, Spanish Rice Seasoning Mix, Seasoned Salt, and Seasoned Pepper. Simmer for about 5 minutes to blend the flavors. Place the fish fillets in a buttered oblong 2-quart baking dish; add the pimientos and olives. Pour the seasoned tomato sauce over the fish. Bake in a moderate oven (350° F.) for 30 to 35 minutes, or until the fish flakes easily with a fork. Makes 6 servings.

SHRIMP RISOTTO

1 cup chopped onion	1 package Lawry's Spaghetti
1 cup chopped celery	Sauce Mix (1½ oz.)
¼ cup salad oil	2 teaspoons Lawry's Seasoned Salt
1 can (6 oz.) tomato paste	2 cups cooked rice
2 cups water	2 cups cooked and cleaned shrimp

Sauté the onion and celery in the salad oil in a large skillet for about 10 minutes. Add the tomato paste, water, Spaghetti Sauce Mix, and Seasoned Salt. Stir thoroughly. Cover and simmer for 25 minutes, stirring occasionally. Add the rice and shrimp to the seasoned mixture. Cover and heat thoroughly, for about 10 minutes. Makes 6 servings.

Note: Two cans (6½ or 7 oz. each) chunk-style tuna may be substituted for the shrimp.

Deviled Shrimp Louisiane

½ teaspoon Lawry's Seasoned salt
½ teaspoon Lawry's Seasoned Pepper
½ cup bread crumbs
1½ pounds shrimp, shelled and deveined
1 egg, beaten
¼ cup butter
1 tablespoon Lawry's Garlic Spread

½ cup finely minced onion
1 can (10½ oz.) consommé
½ cup white wine
2 tablespoons bottled steak sauce
1½ teaspoons dry mustard
½ teaspoon Tabasco
8 ounces green noodles, cooked and drained

Mix the Seasoned Salt and Seasoned Pepper with the bread crumbs. Dip the shrimp in the beaten egg, then in the seasoned crumbs. Melt the butter and Garlic Spread and stir to blend the flavors. Sauté the shrimp in the garlic butter over low heat for 3 to 5 minutes. Remove the shrimp and keep warm while making the sauce. To the browned bits in the pan add the remaining ingredients except the noodles. Simmer until the volume is reduced to half. Arrange the shrimp over noodles. Pour the sauce over all. Makes 6 servings.

Clam Sauce Venetia

¼ cup butter
1 tablespoon Lawry's Garlic Spread
2 cans (7 oz. each) minced clams
½ teaspoon Lawry's Seasoned Pepper

2 tablespoons chopped parsley
8 ounces spaghetti, cooked and drained

Melt the butter and Garlic Spread slowly in a saucepan. Add the liquor drained from the clams and the Seasoned Pepper and simmer for about 5 minutes. Add the clams and 1 tablespoon of the parsley; heat through. Serve on the hot spaghetti garnished with the remaining parsley. Makes 4 servings.

Party Paella Valenciana

2½ pounds chicken breasts, thighs and legs
2 tablespoons salad oil
2 tablespoons olive oil
2 cloves garlic, crushed
1 tablespoon Lawry's Seasoned Salt
1 package Lawry's Spanish Rice Seasoning Mix
5 cups water

2 cups uncooked rice, toasted in oven
4 ounces chorizo, crumbled
2 cans (7 oz. each) minced clams
2 cups boiling water
24 large fresh shrimp, shelled and deveined
1 can (7 oz.) pitted ripe olives, drained
1 package (10 oz.) frozen peas, thawed

Cut the chicken breasts in 4 pieces. Heat the oils in a skillet. Brown the chicken pieces until golden on all sides. Blend the garlic with the Seasoned Salt. Place the Spanish Rice Seasoning Mix in a very large, heavy Dutch oven or kettle (8 quart to 10 quart). Add the 5 cups water, toasted rice, crumbled chorizo, minced clams and garlic - Seasoned Salt paste. Stir thoroughly. Add the browned chicken. Bring to a boil, reduce heat, cover and simmer about one hour. Stir occasionally. Add the boiling water and shrimp. Cover and continue simmering 10 to 15 minutes, until the shrimp are just tender. Then add the olives and peas and let simmer another 5 to 10 minutes. Makes about 12 servings.

Baked Fish with Savory Bread Stuffing and Gourmet Tomato Sauce

Baked Stuffed Fish

1 red snapper, sea bass or trout
(3 to 4 pounds dressed weight)
split in half and boned
Lawry's Seasoned Salt

4 cups Savory Bread Stuffing*
¼ cup melted butter or
margarine

Sprinkle the Seasoned Salt on underside of fillets. Pack Savory Bread Stuffing lightly between the fillets. Fasten the openings with picks or skewers and lace with string. Place the fish in a greased shallow baking pan. Brush with melted butter and sprinkle with Seasoned Salt. Bake in a moderate oven (350°F.) for about 1 hour or until the fish flakes easily. Makes 8 servings.

*Savory Bread Stuffing

¼ cup butter or margarine
½ cup finely chopped onions
4 cups small dry bread cubes

¼ cup finely chopped parsley
1 cup shredded carrots
2 teaspoons Lawry's Seasoned Salt

Melt the butter in a skillet and sauté the onions for about 10 minutes. Place the bread cubes in a bowl. Add the sautéed onions and remaining ingredients. Toss until blended. Makes 4 cups. Note: Bake any remaining stuffing in a small casserole.

Gourmet Tomato Sauce

1 package Lawry's Spaghetti
Sauce Mix (1½ oz.)
1 can (6 oz.) tomato paste

2 cups water
3 tablespoons olive or salad oil
¼ cup red wine

Blend the Spaghetti Sauce Mix, tomato paste, water and olive oil in a saucepan. Bring to a boil, reduce heat and simmer for 25 minutes. Add the wine and simmer for a few minutes more. Serve with baked stuffed fish. Makes 2¼ cups.

Fish

Fillet of Halibut with Shrimp Sauce

3 pounds halibut fillets
2 teaspoons Lawry's Seasoned Salt
1 can (10½ oz.) cream of shrimp soup

¾ cup dry white wine
2 tablespoons minced parsley

Cut the fish in serving-sized pieces and arrange in a single layer in a buttered baking dish. Sprinkle with the Seasoned Salt. Combine the soup and wine; spoon over the fish. Bake in a moderate oven (350° F.) for 30 minutes. Sprinkle with the parsley and serve. Makes 6 to 8 servings.

Rolled Fish Fillets Baked in Savory Sauce

1 package Lawry's Spaghetti Sauce Mix (1½ oz.)
1½ cups tomato juice
½ cup water
2 tablespoons salad oil

½ teaspoon Lawry's Seasoned Salt
1 pound fresh or frozen fish fillets
Lawry's Seasoned Salt
½ cup finely chopped parsley

Place the Spaghetti Sauce Mix in a saucepan. Add the tomato juice, water, salad oil, and Seasoned Salt. Mix thoroughly. Simmer for 15 minutes. Meanwhile, cut the fillets in half lengthwise. Sprinkle both sides with Seasoned Salt. Roll each fillet and fasten with a wooden pick. Place in a 2-quart casserole. Add the parsley to the sauce and pour over the fillets. Bake in a moderate oven (350° F.) for 20 to 25 minutes or until the fish flakes easily with a fork. Serve the remaining sauce in a small bowl. Makes 4 servings.

MARINADES

Marinades have always been a necessity in preparing game, both for tenderizing and flavor. But the modern homemaker has found that delicate marinades can inspire gourmet results in a variety of meat, poultry, seafood and even vegetable recipes. A good marinade can turn a less expensive cut of meat into fork-tender eating and at the same time impart flavor, aroma and color.

Like any seasoning, marinades should be used with discretion. Some foods require hours or days in a marinade, while others are properly flavored in just minutes. Three basic ingredients make up most marinades — oil; an acid such as vinegar, lemon juice or wine; and seasonings, such as herbs and spices, Seasoned Salt, Private Blend Garlic Salt, Private Blend Lemon Pepper Marinade, Seasoned Pepper and seasoning mixes.

Bottled dressings make excellent marinades and basting sauces. Italian Dressing Mix and Lemon Pepper Marinade impart a Mediterranean flair to lamb dishes. Try the Vinaigrette with green beans, tomatoes and zucchini. Delicious and attractive for an Antipasto Tray.

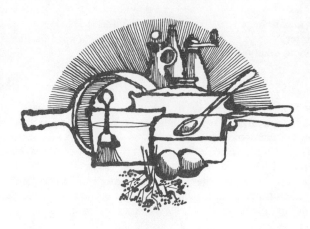

Marinades

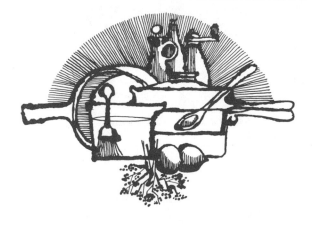

Lemon Pepper Marinade for Flank Steak

1 tablespoon Lawry's Private
  Blend Lemon Pepper Marinade
1½ teaspoons Lawry's Seasoned
  Salt

¼ cup water
½ cup salad oil

Combine the Private Blend Lemon Pepper Marinade, Seasoned
Salt and water; blend well. Add the salad oil and mix. Marinate
a 1½ pound flank steak for 2 hours at room temperature. Use
as a basting sauce while the meat is being broiled. For serving
cut diagonally in very thin slices across the grain of the meat.
Makes about ¾ cup marinade.

Marinade for Shrimp and Scallops

⅓ cup soy sauce
⅓ cup lemon juice
⅓ cup salad oil

¼ cup chopped parsley
½ to 1 teaspoon Lawry's
  Seasoned Pepper

Pour the soy sauce, lemon juice, and oil into a screw-top, pint-sized
jar. Shake well. Add the chopped parsley and Seasoned Pepper and
shake again. Use as a marinade for fresh or frozen shrimp and
scallops. Makes about 1 cup.

Spanish Barbecue Sauce

2 cups tomato catsup
1 cup water

1 package Lawry's Spanish Rice
    Seasoning Mix
½ cup vinegar

Combine all the ingredients in a saucepan. Bring to a boil. Cool. Makes about 3½ cups.

Note: May be used as either marinade or basting sauce. Tasty with frankfurters, spareribs, or shortribs.

Marinade for Lamb Kabobs

1 package Lawry's Italian
    Dressing Mix
¼ cup water
2 tablespoons lemon juice

2 tablespoons honey
¼ cup soy sauce
¼ cup salad oil

Empty the contents of the package into a screw-top, pint-sized jar. Add the water and shake well. Add the remaining ingredients and shake again. Marinate the cubes of lamb for several hours or overnight. Makes 1 cup.

Cranberry Marinade

1 package Lawry's Old Fashion
  French Dressing Mix
2 tablespoons water

¼ cup salad oil
½ cup cranberry juice

Empty the contents of the package into a screw-top, pint-sized jar. Add the water and shake well. Add the oil and cranberry juice and shake again. Excellent for a thick slice of ham or lamb chops. Makes about ¾ cup.

Catsup Marinade-Baste

1 package Lawry's Old Fashion
  French Dressing Mix
¼ cup water
⅓ cup lemon juice

⅔ cup catsup
½ teaspoon Lawry's Seasoned
  Pepper

Empty the contents of the package into a screw-top, pint-sized jar. Add the water and shake well. Add the remaining ingredients and shake again. Use as a marinade or baste on spareribs. Also very tasty on beef, lamb, or chicken. Makes 1¼ cups.

Marinades

Bleu Cheese Wine Marinade

1 package Lawry's Bleu Cheese
  Dressing Mix
2 tablespoons water

¼ cup red wine
½ cup salad oil

Empty the contents of the package into a screw-top, pint-sized jar. Add the water and shake well. Add the wine and oil. Shake again. Use as a marinade on your favorite steak. Makes ¾ cup.

Buttermilk Marinade for Chicken

1 package Lawry's Caesar
  Dressing Mix

2 tablespoons water
1 cup buttermilk

Empty the contents of the package into a screw-top, pint-sized jar. Add the water and shake well. Add the buttermilk and shake again. Allow chicken pieces to marinate for several hours or overnight. Makes about 1 cup—enough for 2½ to 3 pounds of chicken.

Marinade for Beef Kabobs

1 package Lawry's Italian with
  Cheese Dressing Mix
2 tablespoons water
¼ cup red wine vinegar
½ cup salad oil

1 tablespoon Worcestershire sauce
¼ cup chopped onion
1 teaspoon Lawry's Seasoned Salt
½ teaspoon Lawry's Seasoned
  Pepper

Empty the Italian with Cheese Dressing Mix into a screw-top, pint-sized jar. Add the water and shake well. Add the remaining ingredients and shake again. Marinate the cubes of beef for several hours or overnight. Makes 1 cup.

Spicy Ginger Marinade for Chicken

1 package Lawry's Italian
 Dressing Mix
2 tablespoons water
¼ cup white wine vinegar

⅔ cup salad oil
½ cup orange marmalade
2 teaspoons ground ginger

Empty the contents of the package into a screw-top, pint-sized jar. Add the water and shake well. Add the remaining ingredients and shake again. Use as a marinade and baste for chicken. Makes about 1½ cups—enough for 3½ to 4 pounds of chicken.

Wine 'n Garlic Marinade for Lamb

1 tablespoon Lawry's Private
 Blend Garlic Salt
⅓ cup dry white wine

⅓ cup salad oil
2 to 3 pounds lamb cubes for
 kabobs or lamb chops

Combine the Private Blend Garlic Salt, white wine and salad oil. Pour over the lamb. Marinate several hours or overnight. Grill or broil as desired. Makes about ⅔ cup marinade.

Vinaigrette Marinade

1 package Lawry's Italian
 Dressing Mix
¼ cup water

¼ cup white vinegar
¼ cup salad oil

Empty the contents of the package into a screw-top, pint-sized jar. Add the water and shake well. Add the vinegar and oil and shake again for about 30 seconds. Use as a marinade for vegetables such as green beans, zucchini, asparagus, and thick tomato slices. Makes ¾ cup.

Sour Cream Marinade

1 package Lawry's Italian
  Dressing Mix
2 tablespoons water

2 tablespoons lemon juice
½ cup dairy sour cream
½ cup salad oil

Blend together the Italian Dressing Mix and water. Add the lemon juice and sour cream. Combine thoroughly. Slowly add the salad oil, whipping until smooth and creamy. Especially good for chicken. Makes 1⅓ cups—enough for 2½ to 3 pounds of chicken.

Curry Marinade

¼ cup water
¼ cup vinegar
½ cup salad oil
1 teaspoon Lawry's Seasoned Salt

½ teaspoon Lawry's Seasoned
  Pepper
1 teaspoon curry powder

Pour the water, vinegar, and oil into a screw-top, pint-sized jar. Shake well. Add the remaining ingredients and shake again. Use as a marinade and baste for chicken, shrimp, or lamb. Makes 1 cup.

MEATS

The skill of most cooks is generally judged by the excellence of the meat course served. So it is important for today's homemaker to become familiar with the basic facts of buying and preparing a variety of meats, from gourmet steak cuts to pot roast. Your butcher can be most helpful in pointing out the tender and less-tender cuts of meat.

Your eye can tell you a lot about fresh meat. It should have a rich red color with cut surfaces free of moisture. Take a close look at the ratio of fat or bone to the edible meat to minimize waste. Those tiny lines of fat or marbling in the red areas will insure a tender and juicy steak.

Adventuresome seasoning is the secret to successful meat cookery. Spaghetti Sauce Mix adds zesty richness to Barbecued Spareribs, California Pot Roast and Rolled Flank Steak. Seasoned Salt and Seasoned Pepper contribute great flavor to our recipes for Deviled Shortribs of Beef and Pepper Steak. Try Meat Loaf Pizzas for a "different" way to use ground beef. Lemon Pepper Marinade is the "special" seasoning in Lemon Lamb Lawry's — a prize winning recipe.

Continental Beef Stroganoff

1½ pounds beef tenderloin,
  trimmed (about 2 pounds
  untrimmed)
2 to 4 tablespoons butter
1 cup water

1 package Lawry's Stroganoff
  Sauce Mix
1 cup dairy sour cream
2 tablespoons dry sherry

Cut the beef tenderloin crosswise into ½-inch slices. Cut each slice across the grain into ½-inch strips. Melt part of the butter in a skillet. Over high heat quickly pan fry the pieces of beef, a single layer at a time. (The meat should be browned outside, rare inside.) Add the remaining butter as needed. Remove the beef and set it aside. Combine the water and Stroganoff Sauce Mix. Stir thoroughly. Pour into the skillet. Bring to a boil, stirring constantly. Reduce heat, cover, and simmer for 10 minutes. Just before serving blend in the sour cream and sherry. Add the beef and any meat juices. Simmer over low heat just until sauce and beef are hot. Serve with wild rice or buttered noodles. Makes 4 to 5 servings.

BUTTERFLY LEG OF LAMB

1 leg of lamb, 5 to 6 pounds
1 package Lawry's Italian
  Dressing Mix
2 tablespoons water

½ cup Chablis or dry white wine
½ cup salad oil
Lawry's Seasoned Salt

Have the lamb boned and cut open butterfly fashion. Place the Italian Dressing Mix in a screw-top, pint-sized jar. Add the water and shake well. Add the wine and salad oil. Shake again for about 30 seconds. Pour over the lamb in a shallow pan and marinate overnight. Sprinkle generously with Seasoned Salt before grilling. Place the lamb, fat side up, on a grill over hot coals. Grill for 40 to 50 minutes, turning about every 10 minutes and basting with the remaining marinade. Remove from the grill and cut across the grain into thick slices. Serve immediately. Makes 8 to 12 servings.

Note: Leftover grilled lamb may be reheated in foil, or may be used for lamb stew.

Meats

Barbecued Spareribs

4 pounds spareribs
1 package Lawry's Spaghetti
Sauce Mix (1½ oz.)
1 can (8 oz.) tomato sauce
1½ cups water

¼ teaspoon liquid smoke
2 tablespoons brown sugar
1 tablespoon vinegar
¼ teaspoon chili powder
½ teaspoon Worcestershire sauce

Place the spareribs in a shallow pan. Loosely cover with aluminum foil. Roast in a moderate oven (350° F.) for ½ hour. Drain off the fat. Recover and roast for an additional ½ hour. Drain off the fat again. Meanwhile, place the Spaghetti Sauce Mix in a saucepan. Add the tomato sauce and water and blend. Add the remaining ingredients and simmer for 15 minutes. Pour over the spareribs and continue roasting uncovered for about 1 hour. Baste several times. Makes 4 to 5 servings.

California Pot Roast

3 tablespoons salad oil
3 pounds pot roast
2 teaspoons Lawry's Seasoned Salt
1 can (1 lb.) tomatoes
1 cup Burgundy

1 package Lawry's Spaghetti
Sauce Mix (1½ oz.)
¾ cup finely chopped celery
¾ cup finely chopped onion

Heat the salad oil in a Dutch oven and brown the meat slowly. Sprinkle with the Seasoned Salt. Pour the tomatoes and wine over the meat. Add the Spaghetti Sauce Mix and stir until the mix is dissolved. Add the celery and onion. Cover and simmer slowly until tender, for about 2½ hours. Serve the remaining tomato-wine sauce as gravy. Thicken if desired. Makes 6 servings.

Rolled Flank Steak

1½ to 2 pounds flank steak
Lawry's Seasoned Salt
1½ cups Flank Steak Stuffing*
¼ cup flour
1 teaspoon Lawry's Seasoned Salt
½ teaspoon Lawry's Seasoned
  Pepper

¼ cup salad oil
1 can (8 oz.) tomato sauce
1 package Lawry's Spaghetti
  Sauce Mix (1½ oz.)
1 cup water

Have the flank steak scored. Sprinkle it generously with Seasoned Salt. Place the Flank Steak Stuffing at one end of the steak. Roll, skewer, and fasten the meat securely with string so none of the stuffing can fall out. Mix the flour, Seasoned Salt, and Seasoned Pepper together. Roll the steak in the seasoned flour. Heat the salad oil in a Dutch oven and brown the meat. Add the tomato sauce, Spaghetti Sauce Mix, and water. Blend well. Cover and simmer for about 1½ hours or until the meat is tender. Serve the remaining sauce as gravy. Thicken if desired. Makes 4 to 6 servings.

*Flank Steak Stuffing

¼ cup butter or margarine
½ cup chopped celery
½ cup chopped onion

½ cup brown rice
1 teaspoon Lawry's Seasoned Salt
1 cup water

Melt the butter in a skillet. Add the celery, onion, and brown rice. Simmer until the onions are transparent and the rice is browned. Add the Seasoned Salt and water. Bring to a boil, reduce heat, cover, and simmer for about 35 minutes. Makes 1½ cups of stuffing.

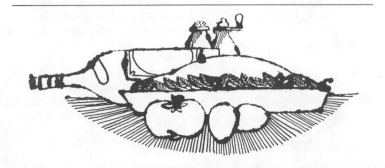

Meats

Miniature Meat Loaf Broiler Meal

1 package Lawry's Meat Loaf
  Seasoning Mix
1½ cups water
2 pounds ground beef
1 package (9 oz.) frozen whole
  green beans
½ teaspoon Lawry's Seasoned
  Salt

1 can (1 lb.) whole potatoes,
  drained
2 tablespoons melted butter
½ teaspoon Lawry's Seasoned
  Salt
¼ teaspoon Lawry's Seasoned
  Pepper
Sautéed onion rings

Blend the Meat Loaf Seasoning Mix with water. Add the ground beef. Combine lightly but thoroughly with a fork. Divide the mixture into 3 equal parts. Shape into loaves. Rinse the frozen green beans under hot water. Place in the bottom of the broiler pan, on the left side. Sprinkle the Seasoned Salt on the green beans. Place the meat loaves on broiler rack on right side. Broil 10 minutes. Brush the potatoes with melted butter. Sprinkle with the Seasoned Salt and Seasoned Pepper. Turn the meat loaves. Add the potatoes. Return to broiler and continue broiling 8 to 10 minutes or until browned. Makes 6 servings.

Meat Loaf Pizzas

1 package Lawry's Meat Loaf
  Seasoning Mix
1½ cups water
2 pounds ground beef

½ cup tomato sauce
1 cup grated Mozzarella cheese
Pizza Toppings*

Blend the Meat Loaf Seasoning Mix with the water. Add the ground beef. Combine lightly but thoroughly with a fork. Divide the mixture in half. Pat into 2 9-inch pie pans. Bake in a moderate oven (375°F.) for 35 minutes. Remove; spread each pizza with ¼ cup tomato sauce. Sprinkle each with ½ cup cheese. Add your choice of Toppings. (*Slices of peperoni, sliced pimiento-stuffed olives, sautéed mushroom slices, chopped onion or green pepper rings in your favorite combinations are suggested.) Place in oven and bake until the cheese is melted, about 5 minutes. Makes 2 pizzas – 6 to 8 servings.

Pizza Pork Chops

8 ounces Mozzarella cheese
8 pork chops, about 1 inch thick, with pocket
1½ teaspoons Lawry's Seasoned Salt
2 tablespoons salad oil

2 packages (1½ oz. each) Lawry's Spaghetti Sauce Mix
1 can (1 lb.) tomatoes
1 can (6 oz.) tomato paste
1 medium onion, chopped

Slice off ¼ of the cheese; grate and set aside. Divide the remaining cheese into 8 equal slices. Stuff each pork chop with a cheese slice. Close each pocket with a wooden pick. Sprinkle Seasoned Salt on both sides of the pork chops and rub in. Heat the oil in a large skillet. Brown the pork chops thoroughly on both sides. Combine the Spaghetti Sauce Mix, tomatoes, tomato paste and onion in saucepan. Bring to a boil. Place the browned pork chops in a large baking dish. Pour the tomato mixture over chops. Cover and bake in a moderate oven (350°F.) for 1 hour. Sprinkle the grated cheese over the cooked chops. Makes 8 servings.

Lemon Lamb Lawry's

2 teaspoons Lawry's Private Blend Lemon Pepper Marinade
1 cup water
2 tablespoons salad oil
2 pounds boneless lamb, cut in 1-inch cubes
1 large onion, sliced
1 tablespoon olive oil

½ cup lemon juice
1 teaspoon Lawry's Seasoned Salt
1½ pounds fresh green beans, cut in 1-inch pieces
1 teaspoon oregano leaves, crushed

Combine the 2 teaspoons Private Blend Lemon Pepper Marinade and water. Let it stand while browning the lamb. Heat the salad oil in an electric skillet at 375°F. Brown the lamb on all sides; add the onion and sauté. Add the olive oil; toss the lamb and onion to coat. Add the water, lemon juice, Seasoned Salt, green beans and oregano. Cover and simmer at 200°-225°F. for 1½ hours, stirring occasionally to prevent sticking. If needed, an additional ¼ cup water may be added during the cooking. Serve over buttered noodles. Makes 6 servings.

Meats

Sauerbraten with Gingersnap Gravy

1½ cups red wine vinegar
½ cup water
1 celery stalk, cut in pieces
1 onion, sliced
2 tablespoons pickling spice
4 pounds boned and rolled
   chuck roast

1 tablespoon Lawry's Seasoned Salt
1 teaspoon Lawry's Seasoned
   Pepper
3 tablespoons salad oil
10 to 14 gingersnaps

In a large bowl combine the vinegar, water, celery, onion, and pickling spice. Place the roast in this marinade and turn several times to coat it well. Cover, refrigerate, and let it marinate for 24 hours. Turn the roast in the marinade several times during this period. Remove the meat from the marinade and wipe it dry. Sprinkle it with the Seasoned Salt and Seasoned Pepper. Heat the oil in a Dutch oven and brown the meat. Add the marinade. Bring to a boil, reduce the heat, cover, and simmer for about 3 hours or until the meat is tender. Remove the meat and strain the marinade to remove the celery, onion, and pickling spice. Measure 2 cups of the marinade and pour in the Dutch oven. Add the gingersnaps and stir until they are dissolved. Simmer for about 10 minutes. Serve the gingersnap gravy over slices of the meat. Makes 8 servings.

Pepper Steak

1 steak (12 to 14 oz.)
1 clove garlic, crushed

1 teaspoon Lawry's Seasoned
   Pepper
½ teaspoon Lawry's Seasoned Salt

Rub the steak on one side with half of the crushed garlic. Then sprinkle with the Seasoned Pepper and Seasoned Salt. Press the seasonings in with the back of a spoon. Turn and repeat. Allow to stand for 30 minutes. Then broil as desired. Makes 1 serving.

Fondue Bourguignonne

2 pounds beef fillet Butter (1 part to 2 parts oil)
Salad oil

Accompaniments: Lawry's Seasoned Pepper, Lawry's Seasoned Salt, minced pimiento, minced parsley and green onion, canned sliced mushrooms, hollandaise or béarnaise sauce, curried mayonnaise.

Cut the fillet into 1-inch cubes. Fill a fondue pot, electric saucepan, or electric skillet ½ full of cooking oil and heat. Add the butter. When the butter has melted and the mixture is hot enough to cook the meat, arrange the container on the table so that the heat may be maintained. Have your guests spear the cubes of meat with fondue forks and cook to their liking in the hot oil. Then have them dip the cubes into the various seasonings and sauces. Add a crisp salad and hot bread or potatoes to complete an exciting gourmet supper. Makes 4 to 6 servings.

Stuffed Hamburgers

1½ pounds ground beef ¾ cup grated Cheddar cheese
1½ teaspoons Lawry's Seasoned 3 tablespoons chili sauce
    Salt 3 tablespoons drained pickle relish

Combine thoroughly the ground beef and Seasoned Salt. Make 10 thin patties with this mixture. Combine the cheese, chili sauce, and pickle relish. Spoon the cheese mixture on 5 of the patties. Top these patties with the remaining patties and seal securely by pressing the edges together. Broil for 3 to 4 minutes on each side, 3 inches from heat, or pan-broil in a skillet over medium heat until well browned. Makes 5 servings.

Meats

Italiaŋ Meatballs

1 pound ground beef
½ pound ground pork
1 egg, beaten
1 large onion, grated
1½ teaspoons Lawry's Seasoned
Salt
½ teaspoon Lawry's Seasoned
Pepper

1 package Lawry's Spaghetti
Sauce Mix (1½ oz.)
3 tablespoons flour
½ cup milk
1 tablespoon butter or salad oil
1 can (8 oz.) tomato sauce
1 cup water

Mix the beef and pork together. Add the beaten egg, onion, Seasoned Salt, Seasoned Pepper, and 1 tablespoon of the Spaghetti Sauce Mix. Mix with a fork. Stir in the flour; then add the milk and continue stirring with a fork to keep the mixture light and fluffy. Chill for 1 hour. Form into 20 medium-sized balls. Heat the butter or salad oil in a large skillet and slowly brown the meatballs. Meanwhile place the remaining Spaghetti Sauce Mix in a saucepan. Add the tomato sauce and water. Stir thoroughly. Bring to a boil, reduce heat, and simmer for about 10 minutes, stirring occasionally. Drain the excess fat from the browned meatballs and pour the spaghetti sauce over them. Cover and simmer for about 20 minutes. Serve over spaghetti, noodles, or rice. Makes 5 to 6 servings.

Note: The browned meatballs may be baked without the sauce in a covered casserole in a slow oven (300° F.) for 20 minutes.

Veal Scaloppine

2 pounds veal round steak or
   cutlets, cut ½ inch thick
¼ cup flour
1 teaspoon Lawry's Seasoned Salt
¼ teaspoon Lawry's Seasoned
   Pepper

¼ cup salad oil
1 package Lawry's Spaghetti
   Sauce Mix (1½ oz.)
1 can (1 lb. 12 oz.) tomatoes
¼ cup red wine

Cut the veal into 6 pieces. Pound to about ¼ inch in thickness. Combine the flour, Seasoned Salt, and Seasoned Pepper. Coat the meat with this mixture. Heat the oil in a skillet and brown the meat. Place the browned veal pieces in a 2½-quart casserole. Add the Spaghetti Sauce Mix, tomatoes, and wine to the oil in the skillet. Stir thoroughly and bring to a boil. Pour over the veal. Cover and bake in a moderate oven (350° F.) for about 1 hour. Makes 6 servings.

Note: Serve the remaining sauce over buttered noodles or rice.

Calves' Liver Italia

1 package Lawry's Spaghetti
   Sauce Mix (1½ oz.)
1 can (8 oz.) tomato sauce
1½ cups water
6 slices bacon
2 medium onions, sliced

½ cup flour
1 teaspoon Lawry's Seasoned Salt
½ teaspoon Lawry's Seasoned
   Pepper
1½ to 2 pounds calves' liver

Prepare the spaghetti sauce according to the package directions, using the tomato sauce and water and omitting the oil. While the spaghetti sauce is simmering, fry the bacon in a large skillet until crisp. Drain and break into bite-sized pieces. Remove all but 2 tablespoons of the bacon fat from the skillet. Sauté the onions until golden. Cover and cook for 5 minutes. Meanwhile combine the flour, Seasoned Salt, and Seasoned Pepper. Coat the calves' liver with the seasoned flour. Remove the onions from the skillet and sauté the liver in the remaining bacon fat. Add the bacon, onions, and spaghetti sauce and combine. Cover and simmer for 5 to 10 minutes. Makes 6 servings.

Deviled Shortribs of Beef

2½ to 3 pounds beef shortribs
1 tablespoon Lawry's Seasoned
  Salt
½ teaspoon Lawry's Seasoned
  Pepper

2 tablespoons salad oil
1 cup water
½ cup red wine
1 medium onion, chopped

Cut the shortribs in serving-sized pieces. Rub with a mixture of the Seasoned Salt and Seasoned Pepper. Heat the oil in a Dutch oven and brown the meat on all sides. Add the water, wine, and chopped onions. Cover and simmer slowly for 2½ to 3 hours until tender. Thicken the pan juices for gravy if desired. Makes 4 to 6 servings.

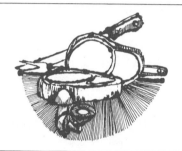

Beef Roll-Ups

2 cups herb seasoned stuffing mix
6 tablespoons water
3 tablespoons butter, melted
3 tablespoons minced onion
2 pounds round steak or cube
  steak, ¼ to ½-inch thick

3 tablespoons salad oil
1 package Lawry's Mushroom
  Gravy Mix
1½ cups water

Combine the stuffing mix, water, butter and onion; mix well. If round steak is used pound with a mallet or edge of a saucer until the meat is about ¼-inch thick. Cut into 6 rectangular pieces. Place ⅓ cup of the stuffing in the center of each piece. Roll up; fasten with skewers or wooden picks. Brown in oil; remove the rolls. Drain fat, add the Mushroom Gravy Mix and water. Blend well; bring to a boil, stirring constantly. Return the beef rolls to pan; cover. Simmer for 2 hours, stirring occasionally. Makes 6 servings.

Roquefort Steak

¼ cup Roquefort cheese
2 tablespoons butter
½ teaspoon Lawry's Seasoned
Pepper

1 teaspoon Lawry's Seasoned Salt
1 tablespoon grated onion
4 steaks (12 to 14 oz. each)

Blend the first five ingredients into a paste and set aside. Sear the meat, turn, and spread with the steak paste. When the second side is cooked, turn and spread again. Makes enough for 4 steaks (12 to 14 oz. each).

Mustard Steak

1 tablespoon Lawry's Seasoned
Pepper
1 teaspoon Lawry's Seasoned Salt

1 tablespoon prepared mustard
1 tablespoon salad oil
3 steaks (12 to 14 oz. each)

Blend the first four ingredients into a paste and set aside. Sear the meat, turn, and spread with the steak paste. When the second side is cooked, turn and spread again. Makes enough for 3 steaks (12 to 14 oz. each).

Hamburgers Italiano

1 pound ground beef
1 teaspoon Lawry's Seasoned Salt
½ teaspoon crushed oregano

2 tablespoons Parmesan cheese
¼ cup catsup

Combine all the ingredients thoroughly. Shape into 4 patties. Pan-broil in a skillet over medium heat for about 3 minutes on each side. Makes 4 patties.

Beef Burgundy Flambé

2 slices bacon
2 tablespoons flour
1 teaspoon Lawry's Seasoned Salt
2 pounds sirloin tip steak, cut in
   bite-sized strips
1 cup Burgundy
1 cup water
1 package Lawry's Beef Stew
   Seasoning Mix

12 small boiling onions
¼ pound fresh mushrooms,
   sliced
16 cherry tomatoes, stems
   removed
¼ cup flaming brandy (100
   proof), optional

Fry the bacon in a Dutch oven. Combine the flour and Seasoned Salt. Coat the meat strips with the seasoned flour. Add the meat to the bacon in the Dutch oven. Brown thoroughly. Add the Burgundy, water, and Beef Stew Seasoning Mix. Stir thoroughly. Cover and simmer gently for 45 minutes. Peel the onions and pierce each end with a fork so they will retain their shape when cooked. Add the onions to the beef mixture and simmer for 40 minutes longer or until the meat and onions are tender. Then add the mushrooms and cherry tomatoes and simmer for 5 minutes longer. If desired, heat the brandy quickly and gently over hot water. Pour the beef mixture into a shallow serving dish. Pour the brandy over the top. Set aflame at the table. Stir gently and serve immediately. Makes 6 servings.

Steak in a Bag

1 sirloin strip steak, 2½ inches
   thick
2 tablespoons Lawry's Garlic
   Spread
2 tablespoons salad oil

1 teaspoon Lawry's Seasoned Salt
2 teaspoons Lawry's Seasoned
   Pepper
1 cup coarse dry bread crumbs

Wipe the steak dry with a paper towel. Make a paste of the Garlic Spread, salad oil, Seasoned Salt, and Seasoned Pepper. Spread over the steak on all sides. Then press the crumbs firmly on both sides of the steak. Place in a brown paper bag and close with a skewer. Bake in a moderate oven (375° F.) for about 45 minutes, for rare. Makes 3 to 4 servings.

Meat Loaf Italia

1 cup bread crumbs
1 package Lawry's Spaghetti
   Sauce Mix (1½ oz.)
1 can (8 oz.) tomato sauce

2 eggs, beaten
1½ pounds ground beef
1 teaspoon Lawry's Seasoned Salt

Place the bread crumbs, Spaghetti Sauce Mix, and ¾ cup of the tomato sauce in a mixing bowl; stir lightly. Add the beaten eggs, ground beef, and Seasoned Salt. Mix lightly with a fork. Shape into an oval and place in a shallow baking dish. Brush with the remaining tomato sauce. Bake in a moderate oven (350° F.) for about 1 hour. Allow to stand for 10 minutes before slicing. Makes 6 servings.

Note: A very easy-to-make and flavorful meat loaf.

Pot Roast Supreme

1 package Lawry's Brown Gravy
   Mix

3 pounds blade pot roast

2 tablespoons red wine
1 medium onion, thinly sliced
Lawry's Seasoned Pepper

Sprinkle the Brown Gravy Mix over the meat. Add the red wine and sliced onion. Wrap securely in foil. Bake in a moderate oven (350°F.) for about 2 hours or until tender. Sprinkle with the Seasoned Pepper. Serve with the gravy. Makes 6 servings.

POULTRY

Some of the most glamorous meals are built around poultry — chicken most frequently. Chicken is a delicate, suggestible meat ready to absorb flavor from wine, sauces, marinades and dressings prior to and during cooking. These treatments also add to the color and crustiness of the outside of the chicken. The exotic aromas emanating from oven, skillet, or coals are among the most persuasive known in cuisine.

Poultry can be handled in so many different ways that it is a joy to work with. It can be boned, floured, marinated, wined, herbed and spiced, fruited and sauced, fried, baked, roasted, barbecued, broiled—whole, halved, quartered or in serving pieces.

A superb dinner, continental style, is easy to prepare with Spanish Rice Seasoning Mix flavor in our Arroz con Pollo recipe. Holiday Roast Turkey with Herbed Cornbread Dressing and Sherried Chicken are popular new dishes — so delicious and easy to prepare, too! For a special dinner party serve Rock Cornish Hens with Wild Rice Stuffing — it's the Seasoned Salt treatment that provides beautiful color and savory flavor.

79

Parmesan Fried Chicken

1 egg
2 tablespoons water
⅔ cup fine dry bread crumbs
⅓ cup grated Parmesan cheese
2 teaspoons Lawry's Private Blend
  Lemon Pepper Marinade

1 teaspoon Lawry's Seasoned Salt
1 broiler-fryer (about 2½ lbs.),
  cut up
¼ cup butter and 2 tablespoons
  salad oil

Beat the egg and water together. Combine the bread crumbs, Parmesan cheese, Private Blend Lemon Pepper Marinade and Seasoned Salt. Dip the chicken pieces in egg, then in bread crumbs. Brown in the butter-oil mixture. Cover; cook 25 to 30 minutes or until tender. Remove the cover during the last 5 minutes of cooking time to crisp chicken. Makes 4 to 6 servings.

Holiday Roast Turkey with Herbed Cornbread Dressing

Use ½ teaspoon Lawry's Seasoned Salt per pound of turkey. Rub the Seasoned Salt inside the cavity and on the outside of the bird. Loosely fill the cavity with the Cornbread Dressing. Skewer openings closed and roast as desired. Baste with melted butter during roasting.

1 pound bulk pork sausage*
1½ cups chopped onion
1 cup chopped celery
4 teaspoons Lawry's Private
Blend Pinch of Herbs

6 cups coarsely crumbled
  cornbread*
¼ cup dry sherry
¼ cup light cream

Cook the sausage meat until crumbly; add the onion and celery. Cook until tender. Drain fat; add the Private Blend Pinch of Herbs, cornbread, sherry and cream. Mix lightly; pack dressing loosely in turkey cavity. Leftover dressing may be baked in a covered casserole. Makes 9 cups dressing, enough for a 14 pound turkey.

*Use a sausage that is lightly seasoned and a cornbread mix with a minimum amount of sugar.

Arroz Con Pollo

1 broiler-fryer (2½ lbs.), cut up
½ cup seasoned flour*
⅓ cup salad oil
1 package Lawry's Spanish Rice
  Seasoning Mix

2 cups water
1 teaspoon Lawry's Seasoned Salt
¼ cup dry sherry
1 cup uncooked rice

Roll the chicken in the seasoned flour. Heat the oil in a Dutch oven and fry the chicken until golden brown on all sides. Remove the pieces as they brown. Empty the contents of the package of Spanish Rice Seasoning Mix into the Dutch oven. Add the water, Seasoned Salt, sherry, and rice; mix well. Place the chicken on top of the mixture. Cover and bake in a moderate oven (350° F.) for about 45 minutes, until the chicken and rice are tender. Makes 4 servings.

*Seasoned Flour: Mix ½ cup flour with 1 teaspoon Seasoned Salt and ½ teaspoon Seasoned Pepper.

Chicken Breasts in Wine

½ cup flour
1 teaspoon Lawry's Seasoned Salt
½ teaspoon Lawry's Seasoned
  Pepper
3 chicken breasts, halved

¼ cup salad oil
¼ cup butter
Rosemary, crushed
½ cup dry sherry

Combine the flour, Seasoned Salt, and Seasoned Pepper. Coat the chicken breasts with the seasoned flour. Heat the salad oil and butter in a medium hot skillet and fry the chicken slowly until golden brown. Remove the chicken from the skillet and place it in a single layer in a shallow baking pan. Pour the sherry over the chicken and sprinkle a pinch of crushed rosemary over each chicken breast. Cover and bake in a moderate oven (350° F.) for 45 to 50 minutes or until tender. Makes 6 servings.

Chicken Pacifica

½ cup flour
2 teaspoons Lawry's Seasoned Salt
½ teaspoon Lawry's Seasoned
Pepper
4 chicken breasts, boned
and halved

2 eggs, beaten
1 cup dry bread crumbs
⅓ cup sesame seeds
¼ cup butter

Mix the flour, Seasoned Salt, and Seasoned Pepper together. Dry the chicken thoroughly and coat with the seasoned flour. Dip the pieces in the beaten eggs and roll in a mixture of the bread crumbs and sesame seeds. Melt the butter in a skillet and sauté the chicken until golden brown. Remove the chicken to a shallow baking dish and arrange in one layer. Bake in a slow oven (325° F.) for 40 minutes or until tender. Makes 6 to 8 servings.

Rock Cornish Hens with Wild Rice Stuffing

¾ cup wild rice
1½ cups chicken stock
3 tablespoons butter
1½ cups chopped celery
½ cup chopped onion

1 teaspoon Lawry's Seasoned Salt
¼ cup sherry
6 Rock Cornish hens
¼ cup butter, melted
1 teaspoon Lawry's Seasoned Salt

Wash the wild rice well; place in a bowl, and add the water to cover. Let the rice soak for 2 hours. Drain the rice; place in a 2-quart saucepan. Add the chicken stock and 1 tablespoon butter. Bring to a boil, reduce heat, cover, and simmer gently for about 30 minutes or until the rice is tender. Meanwhile, melt the remaining 2 tablespoons butter. Add the chopped celery and onion and sauté until crisp-tender. Add the vegetables, Seasoned Salt, and sherry to the cooked rice, mixing lightly to combine. Wash the Cornish hens and dry thoroughly. Stuff each hen lightly with about ½ cup of the rice stuffing; then truss. Blend the melted butter and Seasoned Salt. Brush each hen with the seasoned butter. Roast in a moderate oven (350° F.) for 1 to 1½ hours. Makes 6 servings.

Poultry

Roast Chicken with Giblet Stuffing

1 roasting chicken (4½ to
  5½ lbs.) and giblets
1 celery stalk, sliced
1 small onion, sliced
¼ teaspoon Lawry's Seasoned
  Pepper
5 cups day-old bread cubes,
  toasted
1 teaspoon Lawry's Seasoned Salt

¼ teaspoon Lawry's Seasoned
  Pepper
½ teaspoon poultry seasoning
¼ cup finely chopped onion
2 tablespoons chopped parsley
¼ cup butter, melted
½ cup giblet broth
¼ cup butter, melted
½ teaspoon Lawry's Seasoned Salt

Place the giblets, except the liver, the celery, onion, and Seasoned Pepper in a saucepan. Add water to cover and simmer for about 45 minutes or until tender, adding the liver at the last 20 minutes. Remove the giblets and chop them fine. Save the broth. Toss together the toasted bread cubes, Seasoned Salt, Seasoned Pepper, poultry seasoning, onion, parsley, melted butter, and giblet broth. Rub the body cavity generously with Seasoned Salt. Lightly stuff with the giblet stuffing; then truss. Blend the melted butter and Seasoned Salt. Brush the chicken with the seasoned butter. Roast in a slow oven (325° F.) until a meat thermometer reaches 190° F, or about 2 hours. Makes 4 to 6 servings.

Note: Bake any remaining stuffing in a small casserole during the last 30 minutes of roasting time.

Chicken Cacciatora

2 pounds (approximately 10
  pieces) chicken thighs or legs
2 teaspoons Lawry's Seasoned Salt
¼ cup salad oil

1 package Lawry's Spaghetti
  Sauce Mix (1½ oz.)
1 can (1 lb.) tomatoes
¼ cup sauterne (optional)

Sprinkle the pieces of chicken with the Seasoned Salt. Brown in the salad oil in a large skillet. Remove the chicken and drain off the fat. Blend the Spaghetti Sauce Mix and tomatoes in the skillet. Add the chicken. Cover and simmer for 30 minutes. Add the sauterne and continue simmering uncovered for 15 minutes or until the chicken is tender. Serve over cooked spaghetti or hot fluffy rice. Makes 4 to 6 servings.

Chicken Marengo

1 broiler-fryer (2 to 2½ lbs.),
  cut up
1 teaspoon Lawry's Seasoned Salt
1 package Lawry's Spaghetti
  Sauce Mix (1½ oz.)

½ cup dry bread crumbs
¼ cup salad oil
½ cup sauterne
3 tomatoes, peeled and quartered
2 cups sliced fresh mushrooms

Sprinkle the chicken pieces with the Seasoned Salt. Blend the Spaghetti Sauce Mix and crumbs. Roll the chicken in the seasoned crumb mixture. Heat the salad oil in a skillet to medium hot and fry the chicken pieces carefully. Add the wine, tomatoes, mushrooms, and remaining crumb mixture. Cover and simmer for about 45 minutes or until the chicken is tender. Makes 4 servings.

Grilled Marinated Chicken

1 package Lawry's Caesar or Old
  Fashion French Dressing Mix
2 tablespoons water

1 teaspoon Lawry's Seasoned Salt
1 cup salad oil
2 broiler-fryers, halved

Place the dressing mix in a screw-top, pint-sized jar. Add the water and shake well. Add the Seasoned Salt and oil. Shake again, for about 30 seconds. Pour over the chicken halves. Marinate for several hours or overnight. Place the chicken on the grill, skin side up. Turn the halves every 8 to 10 minutes. Baste frequently with the marinade. Allow about 1 hour. Chicken is done when crispy brown and the drumstick twists out of thigh joint easily. Makes 4 servings.

Sherried Chicken

3 chicken breasts, halved
Lawry's Seasoned Salt, as needed
3 to 4 tablespoons butter
½ cup sherry
1 can (4 oz.) button mushrooms

1 package Lawry's Chicken
  Gravy Mix
1 cup dairy sour cream
Cooked rice

Lightly sprinkle the chicken with the Seasoned Salt. Brown in the butter in a Dutch oven. Add the sherry and the liquid from the can of button mushrooms. Cover and bake in a moderate oven (350°F.) 45 minutes to 1 hour or until the chicken is tender. Remove the chicken to a serving dish. Measure the pan juices and add water, if necessary, to make 1¼ cups liquid. Carefully blend the liquid and Chicken Gravy Mix in a Dutch oven. Bring to a boil, reduce heat and simmer gently for 5 minutes. Stir continually. Blend in the sour cream and add the button mushrooms. When the sauce is smooth and hot, pour it over chicken breasts. Serve with rice. Makes 6 servings.

SALADS
& RELISHES

Salads — a meal in themselves, one course in a meal, or a little side dish — are not only lovely to look at but are an important nutritional adjunct to the diet. A few simple rules for great salads are:

- Buy the freshest greens and buy frequently in order to have on hand daily the basics of a crisp, pretty salad.
- Wash tenderly so as not to break the veins.
- Drain and pat dry or whirl dry in a wire salad basket.
- Arrange the greens loosely in the refrigerator pan so that they may continue to drain while crisping.
- Chill the salad ingredients for 24 hours before serving.
- Break or tear the greens into bite-sized pieces. Cut head lettuce into quarters and then break apart.
- Chill the salad plates, platters or bowls in the refrigerator for at least 5 hours before serving time.
- Chill the salad dressing for 2 to 3 hours.
- Toss the salad or combine the salad ingredients and dressing just before serving.
- Create your own palette in the making of salads. Use colorful garnishes to your satisfaction — hard-cooked eggs, tomato wedges, ripe olives, avocado slices, croutons, sliced radishes, green pepper, asparagus, anchovy fillets.

Relishes impart an added touch of hospitality to any menu. They should be selected as complementary flavors and garnish for entrees or served as delicate flavor contrasts to dishes with bland or pronounced flavors. Try our Luncheon Tostada Salad with Thousand Island Dressing — a hearty dish — fun to serve as a Mexican supper. Marinated Tomato Salad is a favorite with men and ideal to include with a barbecue menu.

Ensalada Granada

1 large celery root (celeriac),
   cooked, peeled, and cubed
½ cup cooked French-cut green
   beans
6 large radishes, thinly sliced
3 large fresh mushrooms,
   thinly sliced
½ carton (about 1½ cups) cherry
   tomatoes, halved
½ bunch water cress, torn into
   sprigs
1 can (2¼ oz.) sliced ripe olives,
   drained

2 tablespoons minced chives
8 thin slices summer sausage, cut
   in julienne strips
1 head iceberg lettuce, quartered
   and torn into bite-sized pieces
Juice of half a lemon
½ teaspoon Lawry's Seasoned Salt
¼ teaspoon Lawry's Seasoned
   Pepper
¾ cup Lawry's Italian with Cheese
   Dressing

Combine the well chilled salad ingredients, except the lettuce and seasonings, in a large salad bowl. Place the torn lettuce on top of the chilled salad ingredients. When ready to serve, toss lightly with the lemon juice, Seasoned Salt, Seasoned Pepper, and Italian with Cheese Salad Dressing. Makes 6 to 8 servings.

Salad Bowl a la Lawry's

This is the famous salad served at Lawry's The Prime Rib Restaurant, in Beverly Hills, California.

1 small head romaine
1 small head lettuce
1 cup endive, torn in pieces
½ cup water cress, torn in sprigs
1 cup shoestring beets, well
   drained

1 hard-cooked egg, sieved
Lawry's Seasoned Salt
Lawry's Seasoned Pepper
¾ cup Lawry's Sherry French
   Dressing

Tear the romaine and lettuce in 2-inch pieces into a salad bowl. Add the endive, water cress, beets, and egg. Sprinkle with the Seasoned Salt and Seasoned Pepper. Toss with the Sherry French Dressing. Makes 6 servings.

Caesar Salad

1 clove garlic	1 tablespoon lemon juice
2 medium heads romaine or leaf	2 tablespoons Parmesan cheese
lettuce (well chilled)	1 cup garlic-flavored croutons
2 anchovy fillets	Lawry's Seasoned Salt
¾ cup Lawry's Caesar Dressing	Lawry's Seasoned Pepper
1 egg, coddled	

Rub a large wooden salad bowl with garlic. Tear 2 medium heads of romaine or leaf lettuce, well chilled, into large pieces; place in the bowl. In a smaller bowl, combine the anchovy fillets with 1 tablespoon of the Caesar Dressing; mash thoroughly. Then add the remainder of the dressing and the coddled egg and blend thoroughly. Pour over the greens. Add the lemon juice, Parmesan cheese, and garlic-flavored croutons. Sprinkle with the Seasoned Salt and Seasoned Pepper. Toss thoroughly. Makes 6 servings.

Luncheon Tostada Salad

1 pound ground beef	1 avocado, cut in thin slices
1 package Lawry's Taco	1 package (6¼ oz.) tortilla chips
Seasoning Mix	1 head lettuce, torn into small
¾ cup water	pieces
¾ teaspoon Lawry's Seasoned Salt	4 ounces Cheddar cheese, grated
1 can (14 oz.) red kidney beans,	1 cup chopped onion
drained	¾ cup Lawry's Thousand Island
4 tomatoes, cut into wedges	Dressing

Brown the ground beef; drain fat. Add the Taco Seasoning Mix, water, Seasoned Salt and beans. Cover; simmer for 10 minutes. Reserve some of the tomato wedges, avocado slices and tortilla chips for use as a garnish. Combine all of the remaining ingredients in a large salad bowl; add the ground beef mixture and lightly toss all of the ingredients. Garnish with the reserved tomatoes, avocado and tortilla chips. This salad is best served immediately. Makes 6 to 8 servings.

Tomatoes Parisienne

1 package Lawry's Old Fashion
  French Dressing Mix
2 tablespoons water
¼ cup red wine vinegar

⅔ cup salad oil
2 tablespoons minced parsley
2 tablespoons minced chives
6 tomatoes, peeled and cored

Empty the Old Fashion French Dressing Mix into a screw-top, pint-sized jar. Add the water and shake well. Add the vinegar, oil, parsley, and chives. Shake again for about 30 seconds. Pour over the tomatoes and marinate for several hours. Makes 6 servings.

Smoky Hot Potato Salad

1 package Lawry's Bacon Dressing
  Mix
⅓ cup water
¼ cup vinegar

⅓ cup salad oil
1 teaspoon Lawry's Seasoned Salt
4 cups cooked diced potatoes
¼ cup chopped green onions

Combine the Bacon Dressing Mix, water, vinegar, salad oil, and Seasoned Salt in a skillet. Add the potatoes and onions. Combine gently but thoroughly. Heat through. Makes 4 to 5 servings.

Celery Root Salad

½ cup dairy sour cream
½ cup mayonnaise
¼ cup light cream
1 tablespoon prepared mustard
1 teaspoon Lawry's Seasoned Salt

1 teaspoon Lawry's Seasoned
  Pepper
2 celery roots (celeriac), peeled
  and shredded (4 to 5 cups)

Combine the sour cream and mayonnaise. Add the cream and whip until smooth. Then add the mustard, Seasoned Salt, and Seasoned Pepper. Blend thoroughly. Pour the dressing over the shredded celery root and toss until well coated. Makes about 6 servings.

Fruit Salad Supreme

1 can (1 lb. 14 oz.) pineapple
chunks, drained*
1 can (1 lb. 14 oz.) sliced peaches,
drained*
1 can (11 oz.) mandarin oranges,
drained

½ cup Lawry's Red Wine
Vinegar & Oil Dressing
1 package (3 oz.) cream cheese
½ cup chopped pecans

Place the fruit into mixing bowl. Pour the Red Wine Vinegar & Oil Dressing over the fruit and marinate in refrigerator for several hours. Meanwhile, cut cream cheese into 16 cubes and roll in chopped pecans and form into balls. Before serving drain the fruit again and garnish with cream cheese balls. Makes 6 servings.

*Fruit juice may be saved and used as a fruit punch base.

Danish Cucumbers

1 medium cucumber
1 teaspoon Lawry's Seasoned Salt

3 tablespoons sugar
⅓ cup vinegar

Slice the cucumbers paper-thin and combine with the remaining ingredients. Refrigerate for several hours or overnight. Makes 4 servings.

Namasu

1 package Lawry's Italian
Dressing Mix
¼ cup water
¾ cup rice vinegar*
2 tablespoons sugar

1 teaspoon grated fresh ginger
1 very large carrot, peeled
2 celery stalks
1 cucumber

Combine the Italian Dressing Mix with the water. Add the vinegar and stir thoroughly. Allow to stand for 1 hour. Meanwhile cut away 5 wedge-shaped strips lengthwise from the carrot. Then cut the carrot in thin slices to form flowerlike shapes. Cut the celery in thin diagonal strips. Cut the cucumber lengthwise and remove the seeds. Then cut in thin slices. Strain the dressing and add the sugar and ginger. Add the vegetables to the dressing and refrigerate for several hours or overnight before serving. Makes 4 to 6 servings.

*A mild vinegar may be used in place of rice vinegar.

Tomato, Onion, and Cucumber Relish

1 package Lawry's Old Fashion French Dressing Mix	2 tomatoes, sliced in thin wedges
¼ cup water	2 onions, chopped
¼ cup vinegar	1 medium cucumber, peeled and sliced
¼ cup salad oil	

Empty the contents of the package into a screw-top, pint-sized jar. Add the water and shake well. Add the vinegar and oil and shake again for about 30 seconds. Place the vegetables in a shallow bowl. Pour the dressing over the top and mix lightly. Allow to marinate and chill thoroughly. Serve as a relish with hamburgers, steaks, chicken, or fish. Makes 2 cups.

Note: This relish may be made in advance and stored in the refrigerator for several days if you wish.

Crispy Cabbage Salad

4 cups shredded cabbage	½ teaspoon Lawry's Seasoned Salt
½ cup chopped green onions, including tops	¼ teaspoon Lawry's Seasoned Pepper
1 cup chopped celery, including leaves	⅓ cup Lawry's Old Fashion French Dressing
¼ cup chopped cocktail peanuts	(made from mix)

Toss the cabbage, onions, celery, and peanuts together lightly. Sprinkle with the Seasoned Salt and Seasoned Pepper. Pour the Old Fashion French Dressing over the salad and toss. Chill thoroughly. Makes 4 to 6 servings.

Salad a la Greque

1 package Lawry's Italian with
 Cheese Dressing Mix
2 tablespoons water
¼ cup red wine vinegar
⅓ cup salad oil
⅓ cup olive oil
18 Greek olives*
½ sweet red onion, thinly sliced

½ cucumber, thinly sliced
2 medium tomatoes, sliced in
 thin wedges
½ green pepper, slivered
8 ounces Greek goat cheese*
 (feta), cut in cubes
1 tablespoon capers, drained
1 teaspoon Lawry's Seasoned Salt

Empty the contents of the package into a screw-top, pint-sized jar. Add the water and shake well. Add the vinegar and oils and shake again for about 30 seconds. Marinate the olives in the dressing for several hours. Combine the onion, cucumber, tomatoes, green pepper, cheese, and capers. Sprinkle with the Seasoned Salt. Pour the dressing with the olives over the salad and toss lightly. Makes 6 to 8 servings.

*Greek olives and Greek goat cheese (feta) may be obtained from a specialty food store. If you cannot locate them, substitute ripe olives and Monterey Jack cheese.

Avocado-Asparagus Green Salad

1 quart head lettuce, cut into
 bite-sized pieces
1 quart romaine, cut into
 bite-sized pieces
½ pound fresh asparagus, thinly
 sliced

1 cup chopped green onions
1 avocado, cubed
Lawry's Seasoned Salt
¾ cup Lawry's Italian Dressing
 (made from mix)

Combine the lettuce, romaine, asparagus, green onions, and avocado in a large salad bowl. Sprinkle with the Seasoned Salt. Pour the Italian Dressing over the salad and toss. Makes 6 servings.

Antipasto Salad

1 can (4½ oz.) artichoke hearts, halved
¼ cup sliced fresh mushrooms
2 tablespoons pimiento strips
1 tablespoon capers
½ cup pitted black olives
1 package Lawry's Italian Dressing Mix*
2 tablespoons water

¼ cup red wine vinegar
⅓ cup olive oil
⅓ cup salad oil
½ bunch water cress
½ head iceberg lettuce
½ head romaine
2 tomatoes cut in wedges or ¾ cup halved cherry tomatoes

Prepare the *antipasto* ingredients and place in a large salad bowl. Combine the Italian Dressing Mix with water in a screw-top, pint-sized jar. Shake well. Add the wine vinegar and oils. Shake again until well blended. Pour over the contents of the salad bowl and marinate for one hour. Meanwhile, prepare the greens for salad. When ready to serve, add the greens and tomato wedges to the marinated vegetables and toss until well mixed.

Optional additions and/or substitutions:

Salami strips, ⅓ cup
Cauliflower pieces, raw or cooked
Anchovy fillets, cut in 1-inch pieces

Pepperoncini, mild Italian peppers
Asparagus, canned or raw

*May be made with Lawry's Caesar Dressing Mix

Sweet and Sour Beets

1 package Lawry's Italian Dressing Mix
¼ cup water
½ cup white wine vinegar

2 teaspoons sugar
1 can (17 oz.) whole or sliced beets, drained

Empty the contents of the package into a screw-top, quart-sized jar. Add the water and shake well. Add the vinegar and sugar and shake again for about 30 seconds. Add the beets and allow to marinate overnight in the refrigerator. Makes 2 cups.

Zucchini Vinaigrette

1 package Lawry's Italian
  Dressing Mix
2 tablespoons water
¼ cup white wine vinegar
¼ cup white wine
½ cup salad oil

2 tablespoons finely chopped
  green pepper
2 tablespoons finely chopped
  parsley
2 finely chopped green onions
3 tablespoons sweet pickle relish
5 or 6 medium zucchini

Make a vinaigrette sauce as follows: Empty the contents of the package into a screw-top, pint-sized jar. Add the water and shake well. Add the vinegar, wine, and salad oil and shake for about 30 seconds. Add the remaining ingredients except the zucchini and shake again. Cut the ends from the zucchini but do not peel. Slice each zucchini into 6 lengthwise strips. Cook in salted boiling water for about 3 minutes. The zucchini should be slightly crisp. Drain and arrange in a shallow dish or pan. Pour the vinaigrette sauce over the zucchini. Marinate for several hours or overnight. Serve on salad greens or on an *antipasto* tray. Makes 30 to 36 strips.

Wilted Lettuce

3 quarts leaf lettuce, torn into
  bite-sized pieces
6 bacon slices
½ cup chopped green onions
⅓ cup vinegar

⅓ cup water
1 package Lawry's Italian
  Dressing Mix
2 teaspoons sugar

Place the lettuce in a large salad bowl. Fry the bacon until crisp, drain, and then crumble. Add the crumbled bacon and onions to the lettuce. Toss. Add the vinegar, water, Italian Dressing Mix and sugar to the bacon fat in the skillet. Heat to the boiling point, then pour over lettuce. Toss thoroughly and serve immediately. Makes 6 to 8 servings.

Salad Nicoise

1 small head iceberg lettuce,
  quartered and torn in bite-sized
  pieces
1 head butter lettuce, torn in
  bite-sized pieces
2 cups cooked, cubed potatoes
1 package (9 oz.) French-cut
  green beans, cooked
1 can (7 oz.) white tuna, flaked
1/4 green pepper, cut in strips
2 hard-cooked eggs, sliced
16 pitted ripe olives

1 small onion, thinly sliced
1 medium tomato, cut in 8 wedges
1 package Lawry's Old Fashion
  French Dressing Mix
2 tablespoons water
1/4 cup red wine vinegar
2/3 cup salad oil
1 tablespoon lemon juice
1 teaspoon Lawry's Seasoned Salt
1/2 teaspoon Lawry's Seasoned
  Pepper

Place the lettuce in the bottom of a very large salad bowl. Arrange the potatoes, green beans, tuna, green pepper, eggs, olives, onion, and tomato in an attractive manner on the lettuce. Combine the Old Fashion French Dressing Mix and water in a screw-top, pint-sized jar. Shake well. Add the vinegar and oil. Shake again. When ready to serve the salad, toss it lightly with the lemon juice, Seasoned Salt, Seasoned Pepper, and Old Fashion French Dressing. Makes 6 to 8 servings.

Ensalada Esmeralda

Zucchini, sliced and parboiled
Lawry's Oil and Wine Vinegar
 Dressing*

Romaine, torn into bite-sized
 pieces
Red or white onion, thinly sliced
Cream cheese, crumbled in chunks

Marinate the zucchini in oil and wine vinegar dressing for several hours. When ready to serve, toss with the romaine, onion and cream cheese.

*Lawry's Oil and Wine Vinegar Dressing:
⅓ cup wine vinegar
⅓ cup salad oil
⅓ cup olive oil**

1 teaspoon Lawry's Seasoned Salt
½ teaspoon Lawry's Seasoned
 Pepper

Combine all the ingredients in a screw-top, pint-sized jar. Shake well. Refrigerate before using. Makes 1 cup.

**All salad oil may be used.

Celery Victor

3 celery hearts
2 cups chicken consomme
1 package Lawry's Old Fashion
 French Dressing Mix
¼ cup water

¼ cup red wine vinegar
¼ cup olive oil
6 anchovy fillets
6 hard-cooked eggs
6 tomato wedges

Wash the hearts of celery without separating the stalks. Trim off the leafy tops so the celery hearts are 6 to 7 inches long. Cut lengthwise into 2 or 4 pieces, depending on size. Place in a shallow baking dish and pour the chicken consomme over the celery hearts. Cover and bake in a hot oven (400°F.) for 30 to 40 minutes until tender but not falling apart. Drain and cool. Empty the Old Fashion French Dressing Mix into a screw-top, pint-sized jar. Add the water. Shake well. Add the vinegar and olive oil. Shake again for about 30 seconds. Place the cooled celery hearts in the dressing, refrigerate, and marinate for about 2 hours. When ready to serve, arrange 1 or 2 celery hearts in a lettuce cup. Garnish with the anchovy fillets, sliced hard-cooked egg, and tomato wedges. Makes 6 servings.

Beets Vinaigrette

1 large onion, sliced and separated
  into rings
2 cans (1 lb. each) sliced beets,
  drained

1 bottle (8 oz.) Lawry's Red Wine
  Vinegar and Oil Dressing

Combine all the ingredients in a shallow dish. Cover; refrigerate several hours or overnight before serving. Makes 4 to 6 servings.

Mixed Bean Salad

1 package Lawry's Italian
  Dressing Mix
2 tablespoons water
1/4 cup vinegar
2/3 cup salad oil
2 teaspoons Lawry's Seasoned Salt
1 can (1 lb.) French-cut green
  beans, drained

1 can (1 lb.) yellow wax beans,
  drained
1 can (1 lb.) red kidney beans,
  drained
1/2 cup minced green pepper
1 large onion, sliced in rings

Empty the contents of the package into a screw-top, pint-sized jar Add the water and shake well. Add the vinegar, salad oil, and Seasoned Salt. Shake again for about 30 seconds. Pour the dressing over the beans, green pepper, and onion rings. Toss lightly. Cover and refrigerate overnight. Serve in lettuce cups if desired. Makes about 8 servings.

Marinated Tomato Salad

5 large tomatoes, peeled and
  sliced
1 clove garlic, crushed
1 bottle (8 oz.) Lawry's Red Wine
  Vinegar and Oil Dressing

3/4 teaspoon crushed oregano
3/4 teaspoon Lawry's Seasoned
  Salt
Lettuce leaves
Chopped parsley

Arrange a layer of the tomato slices in a deep dish. Combine the garlic, Red Wine Vinegar and Oil Dressing, oregano and Seasoned Salt. Pour 1/3 of the dressing over tomato slices. Repeat this procedure two more times. Cover; chill at least 3 hours to blend the flavors. To serve, arrange the drained slices on the lettuce leaves and garnish with chopped parsley. Makes 8 servings.

Basque Salad

6 cups (6 medium) cooked, diced
new potatoes*
1 package (9 oz.) frozen whole
green beans, cooked and drained
1 bottle (8 oz.) Lawry's San Francisco French Dressing
1 teaspoon Lawry's Seasoned Salt

Lettuce leaves
3 tablespoons minced green
onions
1 tablespoon sliced ripe olives
1 tomato, cut into wedges
1 cup julienne ham OR 1 can
(7½ oz.) crabmeat, optional

Combine the potatoes and green beans in shallow dish. Add the
San Francisco French Dressing; cover. Marinate overnight in
refrigerator. Sprinkle with Seasoned Salt. Line a salad bowl with
lettuce leaves; arrange the potato and bean mixture over the
greens. Sprinkle with the green onions and ripe olives; garnish
with the tomato wedges. Add the ham or crabmeat if desired.
Makes 8 servings.

*Cook potatoes in their skins, peel, dice and add dressing while warm.

Luncheon Chicken Salad

1 package Lawry's Old Fashion
French Dressing Mix
2 tablespoons water
¼ cup vinegar
⅔ cup salad oil
4 cups diced, cooked chicken

2 cups chopped celery
½ cup toasted almonds
1 cup halved, seeded Tokay grapes
or seedless green grapes
½ teaspoon Lawry's Seasoned Salt
½ cup mayonnaise

Empty the Old Fashion French Dressing Mix into a screw-top,
pint-sized jar. Add the water and shake well. Add the vinegar
and oil and shake again for about 30 seconds. Pour the dressing
over the chicken and marinate for several hours. Drain the
chicken thoroughly. Combine the chicken, celery, almonds, and
grapes. Sprinkle with the Seasoned Salt. Add the mayonnaise
and mix thoroughly. Makes 8 servings.

Note: This recipe may be cut in half for smaller quantity. Leftover turkey may be used in place of chicken.

SALAD DRESSINGS

It is said that a salad is only as good as its dressing. If true, the dressing should always be "something special." While prepared salad dressing mixes and bottled dressings are excellent as a starter or when in a hurry, just a touch of your own personality can be added to make them great. The secret of using salad dressing mixes is adding water to the seasoning blend first to bring out the full flavor of the spices and herbs.

Often, just a dab of sour cream or a hint of wine makes the difference. New zest is easily added to your favorite dressings with Private Blend Garlic Salt, Seasoned Salt and Seasoned Pepper. For colorful variety, try Confetti Dressing or Roquefort Romaine Dressing and watch your guests perk up when the salad is served.

To insure perfect salads every time, be sure that greens are thoroughly drained, patted dry with paper toweling and crisp-chilled in the refrigerator before serving. Always add the dressing to greens at the last moment, tossing lightly with salad servers to insure that each piece is coated.

In A Pinch Dressing

1 tablespoon Lawry's Private Blend
    Pinch of Herbs
2 teaspoons Lawry's Seasoned Salt

1 tablespoon water
½ cup red or white wine vinegar
1¼ cups salad oil

Combine the Private Blend Pinch of Herbs, Seasoned Salt and water; shake well. Add the vinegar and oil; shake again. Makes 1¾ cups.

Bleu Velvet Salad Dressing

1 package Lawry's Bleu Cheese
    Dressing Mix
2 tablespoons milk

2 to 3 tablespoons dry sherry
1 cup dairy sour cream

Blend the Bleu Cheese Dressing Mix with the milk. Add the sherry and blend again. Then add the sour cream and blend well. Serve over mixed greens or fruit salads. Makes 1¼ cups.

Tivoli Dressing

½ cup mayonnaise
1 cup dairy sour cream
1 cup finely chopped parsley
2 tablespoons tarragon vinegar

1 teaspoon Lawry's Seasoned
    Pepper
1 tablespoon horseradish
1 tablespoon lemon juice
½ cup finely chopped green onion

Prepare the salad dressing by combining all ingredients. Chill for 1 hour to blend the flavors. Makes 2 cups.

©oŋfeʈʈi ᗞreꙅꙅiŋg

1 package Lawry's Italian
Dressing Mix
2 tablespoons water
¼ cup vinegar
⅔ cup salad oil
2 tablespoons chopped green
pepper

2 tablespoons chopped pimiento
2 tablespoons chopped
hard-cooked egg
2 tablespoons chopped pickled
beet

Empty the contents of the package into a screw-top, pint-sized jar. Add the water and shake well. Add the vinegar, salad oil, green pepper, pimiento, hard-cooked egg, and pickled beet. Shake again for about 30 seconds. Serve over wedges of lettuce. Makes 1½ cups.

Avocado Dressing De Luxe

1 California avocado
1 tablespoon lemon juice
½ cup dairy sour cream
2 tablespoons minced parsley
2 tablespoons minced green
onion tops

1 teaspoon Lawry's Seasoned Salt
1 teaspoon Lawry's Seasoned
Pepper
1 tablespoon vinegar
1 tablespoon salad oil

Cut the avocado in half lengthwise; remove the seed and skin. Mash the fruit while combining with the lemon juice. Stir in the remaining ingredients and blend well. Serve over sliced cucumbers, sliced tomatoes, canned asparagus, and canned hearts of celery, separately or in any combination. Keep the dressing covered until ready to serve. Makes 1½ cups.

Note: To prepare for a dip, omit the salad oil and reduce the vinegar to taste.

Orange Cranberry French Dressing

1 package Lawry's Old Fashion
  French Dressing Mix
2 tablespoons water
½ cup orange juice

2 tablespoons vinegar
½ cup salad oil
2 tablespoons whole cranberry
  sauce

Empty the contents of the package into a screw-top, pint-sized jar. Add the water and shake well. Add the orange juice, vinegar, salad oil, and cranberry sauce and shake again. Chill. Serve over fruit salads or with mixed greens. Makes 1½ cups.

Cucumber Cheese Italia

1 package Lawry's Italian with
  Cheese Dressing Mix
2 tablespoons water
1 cup dairy sour cream

½ cup mayonnaise
1 tablespoon red wine vinegar
¼ cup diced green pepper
¼ cup diced cucumber

Blend the Italian with Cheese Dressing Mix with the water. Add the remaining ingredients and blend thoroughly. Chill until ready to serve. Tasty over thick tomato slices or wedges of lettuce. Makes 2 cups.

Chef's French Dressing

1 package Lawry's Old Fashion
  French Dressing Mix
2 tablespoons water
¼ cup tomato juice

2 tablespoons vinegar
1 cup salad dressing or
  mayonnaise

Blend the Old Fashion French Dressing Mix and water in a bowl. Add the remaining ingredients and beat with an egg beater or a wire whip until smooth. Refrigerate and use as desired. Delicious with mixed greens for chef's salad. Makes 1⅓ cups.

Green Goddess Salad Dressing

1 package Lawry's Caesar
  Dressing Mix
2 tablespoons water
1 cup mayonnaise

½ cup dairy sour cream
¼ cup tarragon vinegar
¼ cup milk
⅓ cup finely chopped parsley

Blend the Caesar Dressing Mix and water in a bowl. Add the mayonnaise and sour cream and blend well. Add the remaining ingredients and mix thoroughly. Chill. Serve over mixed greens or wedges of lettuce. Makes 2 cups.

Real George Salad Dressing

1 package Lawry's Caesar
  Dressing Mix
2 tablespoons water
¼ cup vinegar

¼ teaspoon Lawry's Seasoned Salt
1 cup evaporated milk
¾ cup salad oil

Blend the Caesar Dressing Mix and water in a bowl. Add the vinegar and Seasoned Salt and blend well. Add the evaporated milk and oil and beat with an egg beater or a wire whip until smooth. Makes 2 cups.

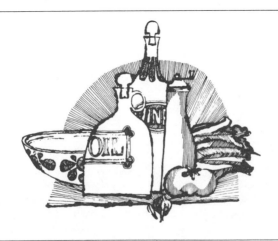

Rum French Dressing

1 package Lawry's Old Fashion
  French Dressing Mix
2 tablespoons water

3 tablespoons light rum
2 tablespoons vinegar
⅔ cup salad oil

Empty the contents of the package into a screw-top, pint-sized jar. Add the water and shake well. Add the rum, vinegar, and oil. Shake again for about 30 seconds. Especially good with avocado salads. Makes 1 cup.

Roquefort Romaine Dressing

2 packages Lawry's Caesar
  Dressing Mix
¼ cup cider vinegar
1 tablespoon lemon juice
¾ cup salad oil

2 tablespoons sugar
¾ cup dairy sour cream
½ cup buttermilk
½ pound Roquefort cheese,
  crumbled

Combine the Caesar Dressing Mix, vinegar and lemon juice; shake well. Add the salad oil; mix well. Blend in the sugar, sour cream and buttermilk. Add the cheese. Chill at least 2 hours to blend the flavors. Makes about 1 pint.

Lemon Italian Dressing

1 package Lawry's Italian
  Dressing Mix
1 tablespoon water

2 tablespoons lemon juice
¼ cup tarragon vinegar
⅔ cup salad oil

Empty the contents of the package into a screw-top, pint-sized jar. Add the water and shake well. Add the lemon juice, vinegar, and oil. Shake again for about 30 seconds. Toss with mixed greens. Makes 1 cup.

SAUCES

The final touch to a well-planned and well-cooked meal is often a classic sauce. Just as the gourmet and restaurant chef know, a fine sauce can make even the most humble dish a work of art. Since sauce cookery indeed is an art, it should be handled with discretion. Limit the use of sauces in a single meal and your choice will stand out, your sense of flavor balance be appreciated.

A sauce should define and complement the dish it accompanies. No matter how perfect the sauce, it should not disguise or cover up the natural flavors of the main dish. The variety of sauces is endless. There are sauces for meats, poultry, seafood, fruits and vegetables. Your own imagination and taste should be the best judge of which sauce to select, but you should start by reading each of the sauce recipes first. You'll find a suggestion for its use in each recipe.

Macadamia Lemon Butter

¼ cup butter
1 teaspoon Lawry's Seasoned Salt
2 tablespoons lemon juice

2 tablespoons chopped
  macadamia nuts

Melt the butter and add the Seasoned Salt, lemon juice and chopped macadamia nuts. Use as a sauce over broccoli, asparagus, or other green vegetables. Makes about ⅓ cup.

Creamy Mustard Sauce

2 egg yolks, beaten
1 tablespoon sugar
1 teaspoon Lawry's Seasoned Salt
2 tablespoons prepared mustard
2 tablespoons vinegar

1 tablespoon water
1 tablespoon Lawry's Garlic
  Spread
½ cup heavy cream, whipped

Place the egg yolks in the top of a double boiler. Add the sugar, Seasoned Salt, mustard, vinegar, and water. Mix well. Cook over the hot water, stirring constantly, until the mixture is thick, about 5 minutes. Blend in the Garlic Spread. Cool thoroughly. Fold in the whipped cream. Makes 1½ cups.

Note: This is a delectable sauce to serve with ham, meat loaf, or green vegetables.

Spicy Cranberry Sauce

1 can (16 oz.) whole cranberry
  sauce
⅓ cup catsup

½ teaspoon Lawry's Seasoned
  Pepper

Mix the cranberry sauce, catsup, and Seasoned Pepper. Heat thoroughly. Serve hot with slices of ham. Makes about 2 cups.

Sauces

Vinaigrette Sauce

1 teaspoon chopped pimiento
1 hard-cooked egg, chopped

1 cup Lawry's Old Fashion French
Dressing (made from mix)

Add the pimiento and hard-cooked egg to the prepared Old Fashion French Dressing. Serve on chilled cooked vegetables such as asparagus, broccoli, and green beans. Makes about 1 cup.

Turkey Barbecue Sauce

2 packages Lawry's Old Fashion
French Dressing Mix
¼ cup water
2 cans (8 oz. each) tomato sauce

2 teaspoons Lawry's Seasoned Salt
¼ cup lemon juice
1 cup salad oil

Empty the contents of the packages into a quart jar or mixing bowl. Add the water and blend. Add the remaining ingredients and mix thoroughly. Use as a basting sauce on turkey while barbecuing. Makes 3½ cups.

Spicy Barbecue Sauce

1 can (8 oz.) tomato sauce
½ cup water
⅓ cup lemon juice
1 teaspoon Lawry's Seasoned
Pepper

2 teaspoons Lawry's Seasoned Salt
1 bay leaf
¼ teaspoon crushed basil
¼ cup molasses

Combine all the ingredients in a saucepan. Simmer, uncovered, for 10 minutes. Remove the bay leaf. Cool. Makes about 1½ cups.

Note: Especially good for basting spareribs, hamburgers, or frankfurters.

Curry Sauce

½ cup chopped onion
1 clove garlic, crushed
2 teaspoons curry powder
½ teaspoon powdered ginger

2 tablespoons butter
1 package Lawry's Chicken
 Gravy Mix
¾ cup water
1 cup milk

Sauté the onion, garlic, curry powder and ginger lightly in butter.
Add the Chicken Gravy Mix, water and milk. Bring to a boil, reduce
heat and simmer, uncovered, 5 to 7 minutes. Stir in bite-size chunks
of cooked lamb, chicken, shrimp or hard-cooked eggs and mushrooms.
Serve over rice. Makes 1¾ cups.

Sauce Laurent

1 package Lawry's Mushroom
 Gravy Mix
1½ cups cold water

2 tablespoons wine such as port,
 sherry, or Burgundy
½ bay leaf

Combine all the ingredients in a saucepan. Stir thoroughly before
heating. Slowly bring to a boil, reduce heat, and simmer, uncovered,
for 5 to 7 minutes until thickened, stirring constantly. When ready to
serve, remove the bay leaf. Serve with broiled hamburgers, meatloaf,
or sliced beef. Makes 1⅓ cups.

Sauce Marengo

1 package Lawry's Mushroom
 Gravy Mix
1 can (1 lb.) tomatoes

1 clove garlic, finely chopped
1 to 2 tablespoons sauterne
¼ cup water

Combine the Mushroom Gravy Mix with the tomatoes and garlic in
a saucepan. Stir thoroughly. Bring to a boil, reduce heat, and simmer,
uncovered, for 5 to 7 minutes. Stir in the sauterne and simmer for 2
minutes longer. Serve with omelettes, sauteed chicken livers, or baked
chicken casserole. Makes 2 cups.

Sauce Bordelaise

2 tablespoons finely chopped
   shallots
2 tablespoons butter, melted
1¼ cups water
½ cup red wine

1 package Lawry's Brown
   Gravy Mix
1 tablespoon lemon juice
2 tablespoons chopped parsley

Sauté the shallots in the butter until they are tender. Add the water, wine, and Brown Gravy Mix. Bring to a boil, reduce heat, and simmer, uncovered, for 5 to 7 minutes. Stir in the lemon juice and parsley. Especially good on roast beef. Makes about 1⅔ cups.

Sauce Bourguignonne

1 package Lawry's Brown
   Gravy Mix
2 tablespoons finely chopped
   onion
1 tablespoon finely chopped
   parsley

2 tablespoons tomato paste or
   tomato catsup
1¼ cups water
2 to 3 tablespoons red wine

Combine all the ingredients except the wine in a saucepan. Bring to a boil, reduce heat, and simmer, uncovered, for 5 minutes. Just before serving, stir in the red wine. Serve with beef or poultry. Makes about 1¼ cups.

Sauce Espagnole

2 tablespoons chopped green
   onion
½ cup grated carrot
2 tablespoons butter, melted
1 package Lawry's Brown
   Gravy Mix

2 tablespoons tomato paste
¼ teaspoon Lawry's Seasoned
   Pepper
1½ cups water

In a 1-quart saucepan, sauté the onion and carrot in the melted butter. When the vegetables are tender, add the Brown Gravy Mix, tomato paste, Seasoned Pepper, and water. Bring to a boil, reduce heat, and simmer, uncovered, for 5 to 7 minutes. A very good basic sauce with many cuts of beef, pork, or veal. Makes 2 cups.

Lawry's Savory Sauce for Fish

1 package Lawry's Spaghetti
Sauce Mix (1½ oz.)
1 can (12 oz.) vegetable juice
cocktail

1 cup water
2 tablespoons salad oil

Blend the Spaghetti Sauce Mix, vegetable juice cocktail, water, and salad oil in a saucepan. Bring to a boil, reduce heat, and simmer for 25 minutes. Makes 2½ cups.

Broiled Fish Sticks: Serve hot over broiled fish sticks or use as a hot dunking sauce with small cubes of the broiled fish sticks.

Oven-Baked Fillets: Excellent sauce for fillets of sole, halibut, or ocean perch.

Baked Stuffed Fish: Ladle steaming hot sauce over whole baked fish and sprinkle with finely chopped parsley just before serving.

Garlic Lemon Butter

¼ cup butter
2 tablespoons lemon juice

1 teaspoon Lawry's Private
Blend Garlic Salt

Melt the butter. Add the lemon juice and Private Blend Garlic Salt. Stir thoroughly. Serve over asparagus, broccoli, Brussels sprouts, carrots, and other vegetables. Makes about ¼ cup.

Lemon Butter

¼ cup butter
1 teaspoon Lawry's Seasoned Salt

2 tablespoons lemon juice

Melt the butter and add the Seasoned Salt and lemon juice. Use as a sauce over broccoli, asparagus, and other green vegetables. Makes about ¼ cup.

SOUPS

For centuries the soup kettle has held a place of prominence in kitchens around the world. How memorable those rich aromas are as the kettle simmers slowly to blend the flavors of vegetables, seasoning blends and hearty beef or chicken broth. What else is as warming and satisfying for the whole family when the weather gets brisk?

Homemakers have discovered that soup is especially popular with youngsters and is economical and convenient to serve. Canned soups with a few added ingredients plus seasoning blends such as Spaghetti Sauce Mix, Seasoned Salt, or Seasoned Pepper produce exciting and hearty soups with that homemade flavor. Fresh vegetables blended with Spanish Rice Seasoning Mix makes a delectable Gazpacho, the classic cold vegetable soup of Spain.

𝕸inestrone

2 cans (10½ oz. each) condensed
  beef consommé
3½ cups water
½ cup lentils
3 bacon strips, diced
1 can (8 oz.) tomato sauce
1 package Lawry's Spaghetti
  Sauce Mix (1½ oz.)
2 garlic cloves
½ teaspoon Lawry's Seasoned Salt
½ teaspoon Lawry's Seasoned
  Pepper
½ cup coarsely shredded cabbage
½ cup elbow macaroni
  (smallest size)
1 package (10 oz.) frozen mixed
  vegetables or 1 can (1 lb.)
  mixed vegetables, drained
  (2 cups)
2 tablespoons finely chopped
  parsley

Pour the consommé, water, and lentils into a large kettle. Add the
bacon, cover, and simmer for 1 hour. Add the tomato sauce and
Spaghetti Sauce Mix. Stir thoroughly. Insert a toothpick into each
garlic clove. Then add the garlic cloves, Seasoned Salt, Seasoned
Pepper, and cabbage. Continue to simmer for 25 minutes. Bring the
soup to a boil and add the macaroni, vegetables, and parsley. Cook
until the macaroni and vegetables are tender, for about 10 minutes.
Remove the garlic cloves. If desired, thin with extra vegetable juice.
Makes 6 to 8 servings.

Hot Tomato Punch

2 cups tomato juice
1 tablespoon Lawry's Garlic
  Spread
½ teaspoon Lawry's Seasoned Salt

Pour the tomato juice into a 1-quart saucepan. Add the Garlic
Spread and Seasoned Salt. Simmer for 10 minutes. Makes 4 servings.

Note: For larger quantity, double the recipe.

Caldo Verde (Portuguese Green Soup)

8 cups water	2 tablespoons olive oil
½ cup chopped onion	1 tablespoon Lawry's Seasoned Salt
6 cups peeled diced potatoes	2 cups shredded cabbage
1½ cups (6 oz.) sliced pepperoni (¼-inch slices)	2 cups shredded fresh spinach

Bring the water to a boil in a Dutch oven. Add the onion, potatoes, pepperoni, and olive oil. Bring to a boil again. Reduce heat, cover, and simmer for 30 minutes or until the potatoes are tender. Remove the pepperoni and set aside. Remove the potatoes and onions and force them through a coarse sieve.* Return to the liquid in the Dutch oven. Add the Seasoned Salt. Bring to a boil and reduce heat. Add the cabbage, spinach, and pepperoni. Simmer for about 2 minutes. Serve immediately. Makes 2½ to 3 quarts—about 8 servings.

*Note: Instead of removing the pepperoni and sieving the vegetables, the soup, at this stage, may be simmered for about 20 minutes longer. At the end of this period, add the Seasoned Salt, cabbage, and spinach. Simmer for about 2 minutes. Serve immediately.

Gazpacho

1 clove garlic	¼ cup minced green pepper
1 package Lawry's Spanish Rice Seasoning Mix	¼ cup minced onion
1 cup tomato juice	2 tablespoons olive oil
1½ pounds fresh tomatoes	1 tablespoon vinegar
1 medium cucumber, peeled and chopped	Lawry's Seasoned Pepper

Cut the clove of garlic in half and rub a large bowl with one of the halves. Empty the Spanish Rice Seasoning Mix into the bowl. Add the tomato juice and stir well. Peel the tomatoes, remove the cores and chop in small pieces. Add the tomatoes, cucumbers, green pepper, and onion to the seasoned tomato juice. Then add the olive oil and vinegar; mix thoroughly. Chill well before serving. Add a sprinkle of Seasoned Pepper. Makes 5 or 6 servings.

Soups

Spanish Rice Soup

½ pound ground beef
2 cups water
1 cup tomato juice

1 package Lawry's Spanish Rice
 Seasoning Mix
¼ cup uncooked rice

In a 2-quart saucepan brown the ground beef until crumbly. Combine the water, tomato juice, and Spanish Rice Seasoning Mix. Add to the cooked ground beef. Bring to a boil, add the rice, reduce heat, cover, and simmer for about 20 minutes, until the rice is tender. Makes 3½ cups, about 4 servings.

Speedy Borsch

1 can (1 lb.) julienne beets
1 can (10¾ oz.) vegetable beef
 soup
1½ teaspoons Lawry's Seasoned
 Salt

¼ teaspoon Lawry's Seasoned
 Pepper
2 tablespoons lemon juice
Dairy sour cream

Drain the beets, reserving the liquid. Place the vegetable beef soup and beets in a 2-quart saucepan. Add water to the beet liquid to make 1 cup and add to the soup and beets. Then add the Seasoned Salt and Seasoned Pepper. Combine thoroughly, bring to a boil, reduce heat, and simmer for about 10 minutes. Add the lemon juice. Top with a dollop of sour cream on each serving. Makes 3½ cups, about 4 servings.

Senegalese Soup

1 cup light cream
1 egg yolk
¼ teaspoon curry powder
½ teaspoon Lawry's Seasoned Salt
¼ teaspoon Lawry's Seasoned
  Pepper
1 teaspoon sugar

1 can (14 oz.) chicken broth
1 can (10½ oz.) cream
  of chicken soup
2 tablespoons finely chopped
  pineapple
chopped parsley

Beat together thoroughly the cream, egg yolk, curry powder, Seasoned Salt, Seasoned Pepper, and sugar. In a saucepan combine the chicken broth and cream of chicken soup. Bring to a boil and remove from heat. Slowly stir in the seasoned cream mixture. Return to heat and cook very slowly for about 5 minutes, stirring constantly. Add the pineapple and chill until icy cold. Serve garnished with chopped parsley. Makes 6 to 8 servings.

Note: Makes 3½ cups.

Hearty Potato Chowder

6 slices bacon, cut in half
1 cup chopped onion
1½ cups water
4 cups diced raw potatoes
1½ cups milk

1½ teaspoons Lawry's Seasoned
  Salt
½ teaspoon Lawry's Seasoned
  Pepper

In a 3-quart saucepan sauté the bacon until crisp. Set aside. Remove all but 2 tablespoons of the bacon fat from the saucepan. Sauté the onion in the fat until tender. Add the water and potatoes and bring to a boil. Reduce heat, cover, and simmer for 15 minutes or until the potatoes are tender but not mushy. Add the milk, Seasoned Salt, and Seasoned Pepper. Crumble the bacon and add to the chowder. Heat thoroughly but do not boil. Makes 6 servings.

Note: For a thicker chowder, cook over low heat for 15 to 20 minutes longer.

VEGETABLES

Served simply or with a delicate sauce or topping, vegetables are a must on every daily menu. Never before have so many vegetables been available to the homemaker virtually the year around. In many cases, seasons are a thing of the past and your family can enjoy their favorite vegetables at any time, fresh or frozen.

The secret of fine vegetable cookery is in cooking them properly and serving them with imaginative seasoning for variety. The Chinese are probably the best vegetable cooks, preferring them slightly under-done or crisp-tender. Vegetables lose texture, color flavor and nutrients when over-cooked. For ideal flavor most vegetables require only butter or margarine and a sprinkling of Seasoned Salt, Seasoned Pepper or Private Blend Pinch of Herbs. A special sauce or topping can turn vegetables into a culinary masterpiece, such as Creamed Spinach a la Lawry's, adapted from famed Lawry's Prime Rib restaurant's recipe.

The artistic cook will select her vegetables both for color and flavor as the right combination can greatly enhance the appearance and flavor of the main course. As a general rule, if more than one vegetable is being served, only one should be prepared with sauce.

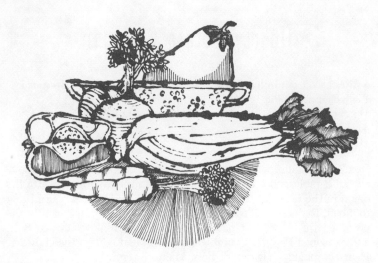

EGGPLANT CHEESE CASSEROLE

1 package Lawry's Spaghetti
  Sauce Mix (1½ oz.)
1 can (8 oz.) tomato sauce
1½ cups water
1 teaspoon Lawry's Seasoned Salt
½ cup finely chopped onion

1 large eggplant
¾ to 1 cup salad oil
½ pound Mozzarella cheese,
  sliced thin
¼ cup Parmesan cheese

Place the Spaghetti Sauce Mix in a saucepan. Add the tomato sauce, water, Seasoned Salt, and onions. Mix thoroughly. Simmer for about 20 minutes. Pare the eggplant and cut into ¼-inch slices. Sauté in the hot oil in a skillet until brown, adding oil as needed. Drain well on absorbent paper. Pour ⅓ of the sauce into an 8-inch-square baking dish. Cover the sauce with the eggplant and Mozzarella slices. Repeat the layers, ending with the sauce, and top with the Parmesan cheese. Bake in a moderate oven (350° F.) for about 20 minutes. Makes 6 servings.

Stuffed Zucchini Boats

6 medium zucchini
1 can (12 oz.) whole kernel
  corn, drained
2 teaspoons Lawry's Seasoned Salt

2 eggs, beaten
¼ cup chopped chives
½ cup grated sharp Cheddar
  cheese

Scrub the zucchini well. Cut off the ends, but do not pare. Cook whole in boiling water for about 7 minutes. Cut the zucchini in half lengthwise. With the tip of a spoon carefully remove the fleshy part of the zucchini from the shells. Chop into small pieces, then combine with the corn, Seasoned Salt, eggs, and chives. Pile the mixture lightly into the zucchini shells. Place in a 2-quart oblong baking dish. Sprinkle with the grated cheese. Bake, uncovered, in a moderate oven (350° F.) for 30 minutes. Makes 6 servings.

Creamed Spinach a la Lawry's

1 package (10 oz.) frozen chopped spinach	1 teaspoon Lawry's Seasoned Salt
2 slices bacon, finely chopped	¼ teaspoon Lawry's Seasoned Pepper
½ cup onion, finely chopped	1 garlic clove, minced
2 tablespoons flour	1 cup milk

Cook the spinach according to the package directions. Drain well. Fry the bacon and the onions together until the onions are tender— about 10 minutes. Remove from heat. Add the flour, Seasoned Salt, Seasoned Pepper, and garlic. Blend thoroughly. Slowly add the milk, return to heat, and stir until thickened. Add the spinach and mix thoroughly. Makes 4 servings.

Creole Stuffed Tomatoes

3 slices bacon	6 medium tomatoes
¼ cup chopped green pepper	1 cup whole kernel corn
¼ cup chopped onion	1 teaspoon Lawry's Seasoned Salt

Fry the bacon in a skillet until crisp. Drain and set aside. Remove the drippings, leaving about 1 tablespoon. Sauté the green pepper and onion slightly. Meanwhile prepare the tomatoes by removing the top slice and center core from each. Scoop out the pulp and break it up. Add the pulp, corn, and Seasoned Salt to the vegetables in the skillet. Heat thoroughly. Crumble the bacon and add to the vegetable mixture, saving out some of the bacon for garnish. Fill the tomato cups and top with the remaining bacon. Bake in a shallow dish in a moderate oven (350° F.) for 15 to 20 minutes. Makes 6 servings.

GERMAN STYLE CABBAGE AND BEANS

6 slices bacon
6 cups thinly shredded cabbage
1 cup white wine vinegar
2 tablespoons sugar*

1 tablespoon Lawry's Private
    Blend Garlic Salt
2 cans (1 lb. each) French-cut
    green beans, drained

Fry the bacon until crisp; drain on paper towel. Add the cabbage, vinegar, sugar and Private Blend Garlic Salt to the bacon drippings; cover. Cook for 5 minutes or until the cabbage is tender. Crumble the bacon; add to the cabbage along with the green beans. Heat thoroughly. Makes 6 servings.

*For a sweeter flavor, increase sugar to ¼ cup.

Oriental Celery Sauté

2 tablespoons butter
2 cups diagonally sliced celery
½ cup diagonally sliced green
    onions
1 can (4 oz.) sliced mushrooms,
    drained

1 can (5 oz.) water chestnuts,
    drained and sliced
1 teaspoon Lawry's Seasoned Salt
¼ teaspoon Lawry's Seasoned
    Pepper

Melt the butter in a skillet. Add the remaining ingredients and sauté for 2 minutes until crisp-tender, stirring constantly. Makes 4 servings.

CALIFORNIA CORN CASSEROLE

2 packages (10 oz. each)
frozen whole kernel corn
2 eggs, beaten
1 cup light cream
½ cup cracker crumbs
1 teaspoon Lawry's Seasoned Salt

½ teaspoon Lawry's Seasoned
Pepper
1 can (2¼ oz.) sliced ripe olives
3 ounces Swiss cheese,
cut in strips
3 bacon slices, halved

Cook the corn according to the package directions, omitting the salt. Combine the eggs, cream, cracker crumbs, Seasoned Salt, Seasoned Pepper, and olives. Drain the corn thoroughly and add to the egg mixture. Pour into a buttered 2-quart casserole. Place the strips of cheese over the corn mixture and the bacon halves on top of the cheese. Bake in a moderate oven (350° F.) for 30 to 40 minutes or until the bacon is fairly crisp. Sprinkle with the Seasoned Pepper. Makes 6 servings.

ZUCCHINI CUSTARD

1 medium onion, sliced
2 tablespoons butter
1 pound zucchini
2 teaspoons Lawry's Seasoned Salt
½ teaspoon Lawry's Seasoned
Pepper

6 eggs
1 cup milk
½ pound Mozzarella cheese,
sliced

Sauté the onions in the butter for about 10 minutes. Slice the unpeeled zucchini into ½-inch slices. Add the zucchini, Seasoned Salt, and Seasoned Pepper to the onions and sauté for about 5 minutes. Beat the eggs slightly. Stir in the milk. Then add the vegetable mixture. Pour into a buttered 2-quart oblong baking dish. Set the dish in a pan of hot water. Bake in a slow oven (300° F.) for 25 minutes. Then top with the Mozzarella cheese slices. Bake for another 25 minutes or until the custard is firm. Make 6 to 8 servings.

Vegetables

Potatoes Au Gratin

1 package (12 oz.) frozen hash brown potatoes, defrosted	½ teaspoon Lawry's Seasoned Pepper
1 cup milk	1 teaspoon Lawry's Seasoned Salt
2 tablespoons butter	¼ cup sliced green onion
	1½ cups grated Cheddar cheese

Preheat the oven to 350° F. Spread the potatoes evenly in a shallow casserole. Scald the milk with the butter, Seasoned Pepper, and Seasoned Salt. Sprinkle the onions and cheese over the potatoes and pour on the milk and seasonings. Bake, covered, for 25 to 30 minutes. Makes 4 servings.

Potatoes in Armor

4 medium baking potatoes, peeled	1 teaspoon Lawry's Seasoned Pepper
½ cup softened butter	
2 teaspoons Lawry's Seasoned Salt	

Cut the potatoes in ½-inch slices crosswise. Blend together the softened butter, Seasoned Salt, and Seasoned Pepper. Spread about 2 tablespoons of the seasoned butter mixture between the potato slices. Wrap in aluminum foil, closing securely. Arrange on the barbecue grill over medium heat. Cook for 30 minutes; turn and cook for 30 minutes longer. Makes 4 servings.

Open Face Summer Squash

8 summer squash	1 teaspoon Lawry's Seasoned Salt
½ cup water	½ cup grated Cheddar cheese
2 tablespoons butter	

Cut the squash in half crosswise and steam cook for about 10 minutes. Arrange cut side up in a 3-quart oblong baking dish. Melt the butter and add the Seasoned Salt; drizzle over the cut squash. Pierce the center of each squash so that the seasoned butter is absorbed. Bake in a moderate oven (350° F.) for about 20 minutes. Top with the grated cheese and continue baking for about 10 minutes until the cheese melts. Makes about 8 servings.

Company Carrot Casserole

¼ cup butter
1 small onion, minced
¼ cup flour
1 teaspoon Lawry's Seasoned Salt
¼ teaspoon Lawry's Seasoned
  Pepper

2 cups milk
4 cups diagonally sliced carrots,
  cooked and drained
6 slices American cheese
2 cups buttered fresh bread
  crumbs

Melt the butter in a saucepan and saute' the onion. Stir in the flour, Seasoned Salt and Seasoned Pepper. Gradually add the milk, stirring constantly. Arrange a layer of carrots in the bottom of a 2-quart casserole. Place 3 slices of cheese over the carrots. Repeat the layers. Pour the sauce over the carrots. Top with the bread crumbs. Bake, uncovered, in a moderate oven (350°F.) for 25 minutes. Makes 6 to 8 servings.

Refried Beans

1 can (1 lb. 4 oz.) refried beans
1 package Lawry's Taco Seasoning
  Mix

¼ cup water
¾ cup grated mild Cheddar cheese
¼ cup finely chopped onions

Combine the refried beans, Taco Seasoning Mix and water in a saucepan. Bring to a boil, reduce heat and simmer for 5 minutes. Garnish the bean mixture with the grated cheese and the chopped onions just before serving. Makes 2½ cups or 5 servings.

Carrots Vichy

2 cups sliced raw carrots
½ cup boiling water
2 tablespoons butter, melted
1 teaspoon lemon juice

½ teaspoon Lawry's Seasoned Salt
¼ teaspoon Lawry's Seasoned
  Pepper
Finely chopped parsley

Cook the carrots in the boiling water until they are just tender. Mix together the melted butter, lemon juice, Seasoned Salt, and Seasoned Pepper. Pour over the carrots and toss lightly. Sprinkle with the finely chopped parsley. Makes 4 servings.

ABOUT MENUS

There's artistry and adventure in planning interesting menus. It is fun and rewarding too, when you see family and guests enjoy the results of your thoughtful planning and preparation. Here are a few pointers.

First of all, the occasion should be considered. Holiday dinners and special parties deserve extra attention in selecting colorful and appetizing flavor combinations. Table decorations related to the theme of the menu add extra flair. For casual family meals on busy days, choose favorites that are easy to prepare and sure to be accepted. For entertaining, try something really different!

Next, the flavor and texture of foods should complement each other. With mild or bland flavored casseroles, serve tart and crisp green salads. With spicy meats or main dishes, serve a delicate fruit salad and mildly seasoned vegetables. Breads and sauces are also important for menu variety.

Making a schedule for preparation and cooking time is very helpful. Start the longest cooking dish first. Then gauge the other recipe cooking times accordingly so that each dish will be ready to serve at the right time.

The menu suggestions presented here were created to help a busy homemaker serve flavorful, attractive and distinctive meals — sure to delight both her family and guests —for a variety of occasions.

Pennsylvania Dutch Dinner

Hearty hospitality and love of life expressed in the robust fare of the Pennsylvania Dutch country — fork-tender Sauerbraten and its famous side dishes to welcome you to the table.

Sauerbraten
with
Gingersnap Gravy[1]

Potatoes Au Gratin[2]

German Style Cabbage and Beans[2]

Applesauce

Black Bread with Butter

Linzer Torte

[1]See Meats
[2]See Vegetables

East Indian Dinner

A beautiful Shrimp Curry dinner appropriate to warm-weather months, drawn from the exotic cuisine of the East Indies but composed of familiar, easily handled foods.

Shrimp Curry[1]

Fluffy White Rice

Chopped Hard-Cooked Egg   Toasted Coconut

Crisp Bacon Bits   Mandarin Oranges   Chutney

Raisins   Almonds or Peanuts

Baked Bananas

Key Lime Pie

[1]See Fish

VIP Dinner Party

Rock Cornish Hens are elegant for a special occasion and become the center attraction for a memorable dinner.

Rock Cornish Hens
with
Wild Rice Stuffing[1]

Carrots Vichy[2]

Belgian Endive Salad
with
Bleu Velvet Salad Dressing[3]

Hot Rolls

Strawberries Romanoff or Cherries Jubilee

[1]See Poultry
[2]See Vegetables
[3]See Salad Dressings

Friday Fare

A change of pace casserole, Magyar Eggplant, is a pleasant choice for Friday or any day, with Herb Seasoned Bread to add flavor to the meal, Tossed Green Salad for color and texture contrast, and Chocolate Frosted Brownies for a sweet ending.

Magyar Eggplant[1]

Herb Seasoned Bread[2]

Tossed Green Salad with Lemon Italian Dressing[3]

Chocolate Frosted Brownies

[1]See Casseroles and Entrees
[2]See Seasoned Hot Breads
[3]See Salad Dressings

Green Pepper Pieces

BRIDGE LUNCHEON FOR THE GIRLS

Basque Salad was inspired by the sturdy people of the same name. Hearty and delicious, the vegetables are marinated ahead and tossed with the remaining ingredients just before serving. Simple but elegant fare!

Basque Salad[1]

Hot Crusty Rolls

Lemon Chiffon Pie

[1]See Salads and Relishes

Balance The Budget

Economy combined with imagination can be a gustatorial triumph with these delicious, low-cost Deviled Shortribs of Beef and tasty go-withs in exciting variety.

Deviled Shortribs of Beef[1]

Baked Potatoes

Buttered Green Beans   Sweet and Sour Beets[2]

Pepper Bread Sticks[3]

Apple Crisp

[1]See Meats
[2]See Salads and Relishes
[3]See Seasoned Hot Breads

Gourmet Supper

The makings of an important little supper — Fondue Bourguignonne with long fondue forks for the cooking and dipping into the savory sauces and the Continental touch of crusty French Bread.

Fondue Bourguignonne[1]
Creamy Mustard Sauce[2]
Sauce Bordelaise[2]
Sauce Espagnole[2]
Marinated Tomato Salad[3]
Sliced French Bread
Chocolate Mousse

[1]See Meats
[2]See Sauces
[3]See Salads and Relishes

Sunday Night Supper

Scotch Rarebit and Grilled Canadian Bacon, two favorites in distinctive flavors both contrasting and compatible. They make a light supper irresistible to appetites high after the weekend's last swim and final romp with the dogs.

Scotch Rarebit[1]

Grilled Canadian Bacon

Fresh Fruit Cup   Cookies

[1]See Eggs and Cheese

Menus

₲OLD-WEATHER PIƆNIƆ

Served indoors before the fire in the cabin or out in the winter sunshine, this cold-weather picnic spread of Barbecued Beef on Toasted Buns will lift the spirits of happy wanderers—perhaps even inspire wanderlust in the most comfortable stay-at-home.

Barbecued Beef[1] on Toasted Buns

Crispy Cabbage Salad[2]

Fresh Fruit in Season   Cookies

Hot Spiced Cider

[1] See Casseroles and Entrees
[2] See Salads and Relishes

ℳexican ℱiesta Supper

Famous Gazpacho, Spanish cold soup, leads the way in this festive, south-of-the-border supper made up of delectable choices from the Mexican *cocina*.

Gazpacho[1]

Enchiladas Rancheros[2]

Mexican Fried Rice[3]

Refried Beans[4]

Lime Ice

[1] See Soups
[2] See Casseroles and Entrees
[3] See Casseroles and Entrees
[4] See Vegetables

Stag Barbecue

Fare for the mighty hunter and his gun club, golf partners, friends from the sports car crowd. Steak in three man-pleasing guises, with classic accompaniments.

Steak Trio:

Mustard Steak[1]   Pepper Steak[1]   Roquefort Steak[1]

Baked Potato   Caesar Salad[2]

Sourdough French Bread

Apple Pie with Cheese

[1]See Meats
[2]See Salads and Relishes

Backyard Barbecue

Richly golden and aromatic, Grilled Marinated Chicken is all the more beguiling amidst the splendors of the garden. The barbecue is a huge success as hungry guests help themselves to this special chicken, marinated in salad dressing for special flavor. Then on to Potatoes in Armor and Beets Vinaigrette.

Grilled Marinated Chicken[1]

Potatoes in Armor[2]

Beets Vinaigrette[3]

Fresh Strawberry Shortcake

[1]See Poultry
[2]See Vegetables
[3]See Salads and Relishes

Barbecue for Company

Mysteries of the Near East and the Mediterranean, too, solved at barbecue time before the eyes of admiring guests as Butterfly Leg of Lamb roasts to a turn on the grill and Rice Pilaf awaits fragrantly nearby.

Butterfly Leg of Lamb[1]

Rice Pilaf

Tomatoes Parisienne[2]

Buttered Hot Rolls

Crème de Menthe Parfait

[1]See Meats
[2]See Salads and Relishes

Family Get~Together Picnic

It's always fair weather when hungry picnickers get together. To fill the picnic plate balanced on your knee—handsome Barbecued Spareribs and easily assembled accompaniments like Potato Salad, Mixed Bean Salad, Corn-on-the-Cob, and Homemade Ice Cream.

Barbecued Spareribs[1]

Potato Salad   Mixed Bean Salad[2]

Corn-on-the-Cob

Homemade Ice Cream

[1]See Meats
[2]See Salads and Relishes

Menus

Fiesta Luncheon or Supper Salad

Piping hot taco seasoned meat is tossed with crisp salad greens and vegetables to prepare this unique Tostada Salad. The men in your family will enjoy this hearty salad too.

Luncheon Tostada Salad[1]
Warm Buttered Tortillas
Choice of Ice Cream with Fresh Fruit
Mexican Beer

[1]See Salads and Relishes

Happy Holiday Dinner

The holiday bird, roasted to golden perfection, is enhanced by the addition of Seasoned Salt and lots of melted butter for basting. The rest of the menu rounds out the family get-together.

Hot Tomato Punch[1]
Holiday Roast Turkey with Herbed Cornbread Dressing[2]
Celery Victor[3]
Cranberry Relish
Company Carrot Casserole[4]
Pepper Bread Sticks[5]
Pumpkin, Mincemeat or Pecan Pie

[1]See Soups
[2]See Poultry
[3]See Salads and Relishes
[4]See Vegetables
[5]See Seasoned Hot Breads

INDEX

LAWRY'S

Home Savings, in conjunction with Lawry's Foods, Inc.,
has enjoyed bringing you this special edition of
"Cooking Secrets Your Mother Never Told You!",
as created by the Consumer Services staff
of Lawry's Foods, Inc.